Weighing up the Evidence

HOW AND WHY:

The American Revolution

Erica Holley

Dryad Press Limited London

Contents

ACKNOWLEDGMENTS

The author would like to thank the following for their help in the preparation of this book: Sarah Harris, Nick Harris, Betty Holley, Barbara Mitchell, Ruth Taylor and Chris Walton.

The author and publishers would like to thank the following for their permission to reproduce illustrations: BBC Hulton Picture Library, pages 15, 18; the Trustees of the British Museum, pages 16, 44, 52; Culver Pictures, Inc, page 37; Mary Evans Picture Library, page 11; The Fotomas Index, page 38; The Mansell Collection, pages 13, 22, 24, 40, 43; National Maritime Museum, London, page 45; National Portrait Gallery, London, pages 21, 26; Peter Newark's Western Americana, pages 7, 30. The maps on pages 3, 9 and 27 were drawn by R.F. Brien.

The colour picture on the front cover is "The Spirit of '76" by A.M. Willard (Peter Newark's Western Americana). The black and white pictures show Washington crossing the Delaware, 12 December 1776 (Mary Evans Picture Library) and the Boston Massacre, by Paul Revere (The Mansell Collection).

© Erica Holley 1986   First published 1986
Typeset by Tek-Art Ltd, Kent
and printed in Great Britain by R J Acford Ltd, Chichester, Sussex
for the Publishers, Dryad Press Limited,
4 Fitzhardinge Street, London W1H 0AH

Introduction

In the late fifteenth century, while trying to discover new sea routes to the East, European sailors learnt that the American continent existed. There followed two centuries of exploration and settlement in this "New World" by Europe, with Spain, France and Britain gaining control over large areas of North America. The Spanish Empire was in the far west, Florida and Mexico; France controlled a series of outposts from Canada through the Mississippi to New Orleans. The first permanent British settlement was established in 1607 at Jamestown, Virginia. British colonies were founded, with royal permission, by chartered companies concerned with trade, by religious groups wishing to set up new communities outside Britain, or by men who were granted large amounts of American land by the British Crown.

By 1733 there were thirteen British colonies, each with its own Royal

The thirteen colonies.

Charter. In order of their founding they were Virginia, Massachusetts, New Hampshire, New York, Connecticut, Maryland, Rhode Island, Delaware, Pennsylvania, North Carolina, New Jersey, South Carolina and Georgia. In competition for Empire, Britain fought her rivals, France and Spain, on various occasions in the early eighteenth century. The Seven Years War (1756-63) was fought partly in Canada. Britain gained victory in that war and in the Peace of Paris France ceded Canada and Spain ceded Florida to Britain. Thus, in the mid-eighteenth century, British colonies stretched from Quebec in the north to East Florida in the south.

The colonies were not united but were more like individual nations, with their own governments and economic, religious and cultural identities. Their strongest link was allegiance to the British Crown. As part of the British Empire the colonies accepted Britain's control of their trade and her protection against hostile Indian tribes and world powers who wished to extend their influence on the American continent.

Success in the Seven Years War brought economic problems for Britain. The national debt had doubled by 1763 and the costs of defending and administering a growing Empire were crippling and increasing. In 1764 the British government began to levy a series of taxes on the American colonies. The taxes were designed to raise money to cover the costs of the Empire in North America. Until 1764 Britain had taxed the Americans only indirectly in the form of customs duties. As the colonists had never been directly taxed by Britain, they denied the right of Parliament to impose the new taxes. Since colonists were not represented in the British Parliament, they resisted taxation on the principle that they could be taxed only by their own representatives.

The twelve years after 1764 were a time of crisis in British-American relations as each side tried to assert its view of how an Empire should be run. During this period the original thirteen colonies began to act together in their dispute with Britain and in 1776 they declared their independence as united colonies. Their union was weak and uncertain and they had no long-term plans for the future. They were sure of only one thing: that they wished independence from the British Empire.

The Declaration of Independence on 4 July 1776 can be seen as the start of the American Revolution. The Declaration was startling because it was so final. Before, reconciliation or compromise between the British Parliament and the colonies was a possibility, however remote. The Declaration of Independence showed that colonists rejected Imperial rule; compromise was no longer possible and war could be the only result. Britain had lost control of her American Empire and had either to fight to regain it or to agree to a new independent state.

The war of independence which followed was a vital part of the revolution: independence might have been declared but the war was necessary to secure it. Fighting between American and British armies lasted until a humiliating British defeat at Yorktown at the end of 1781, but British troops did not finally leave American soil until late 1783 when peace had been confirmed by the Treaty of Paris.

As well as being a war for independence, the American Revolution was a political revolution concerned with power and ideas of liberty. Americans claimed to be defending long-held liberties and freedom from the arbitrary rule of a British King and Parliament. It was certainly not a social revolution: no new class came to power; voting rights remained restricted to white, male, property owners; and slavery continued.

The American struggle for independence is still a controversial subject among historians; some even maintain that there was no revolution because nothing really changed in the colonies after the British left. The American historian Robert Palmer wrote: "The British lid may have been removed from the American box, with the contents remaining as before".

Twentieth-century historians must be careful in making judgements about how real the American Revolution was, because ideas of what a revolution is or should be have changed so much since 1776. In contrast to the French Revolution of 1789, which resulted in a reign of terror, mass executions, including the execution of the King, and the uprising of the lowest classes, the American Revolution, directed and controlled by wealthy merchants, farmers and lawyers and with no mass executions, may seem unexciting. Those involved in it had no doubt that they were taking part in a revolutionary event: the dismissal of British power from the thirteen colonies and the establishment of a new republican state.

The purpose of this book is to investigate the causes and motives that led to the American Revolution and explain why it succeeded. It examines evidence from a variety of sources and explores ideas and explanations in an attempt to establish the causes of the Revolution.

When reading the extracts from the different kinds of evidence it is important to be aware that the war of independence was not a simple one of rebel Americans against Imperial Britons. There were loyalist men and women in America who did not support the revolution. In Britain there was widespread opposition to the government's American policies.

In assessing the importance of political and military events on both sides of the Atlantic, it is also worth remembering that news, orders and supplies had to cross that ocean and could take six weeks to arrive. News of the decisive British defeat at Yorktown on 8 October 1781 was not brought to the British Prime Minister until 25 November.

At the end of the book you will find a number of important sections to which you should refer as you work through the main chapters. The Biographies on pages 58-60 will help you to understand the kind of people who were making decisions at the time; they may enable you to understand why these decisions were made. The Glossary explains some of the difficult words used in the extracts.

In 1815, John Adams, who was a revolutionary in 1776 and became the second President of the United States in 1796, wrote: "Who shall write the History of the American Revolution? Who can write it? Who will ever be able to write it?" The job of an historian is to try to understand such important events as the American Revolution; the first step is to understand how the Revolution happened and why people acted as they did.

The Story of the Revolution

To tell the full story of the Revolution with all the details of the battles and campaigns would not be possible. This chapter simply traces the important events of the war years, looking at the evidence left by the people involved.

The chapter begins with the drafting of the Declaration of Independence in June 1776 and its approval by the Second Continental Congress which had delegates from the original thirteen colonies: Virginia, Massachusetts, New Hampshire, New York, Connecticut, Maryland, Rhode Island, Delaware, Pennsylvania, North Carolina, New Jersey, South Carolina and Georgia. Each colony had instructed its delegates to vote for independence. The remaining British colonies in North America stayed loyal to Britain. Twelve of the colonies, without Georgia, had met before in September 1774 in the First Continental Congress: this had petitioned the King, George III, for help in reaching a reasonable solution to the disagreements between the colonies and the British Parliament, without success.

Fighting between British troops and Americans had already broken out in some areas in April 1775. In the following month the Second Continental Congress had appointed George Washington as Commander-in-Chief of the Continental Army. The army had not yet been formed and Washington's first job was to create it. In August 1775 George III had declared the colonies to be in rebellion. In March 1776 British troops had evacuated Boston and withdrawn to Nova Scotia. Royal Governors no longer had effective authority in any colony by June 1776, as colonial assemblies had assumed power in their own right and discarded the old colonial system. A proclamation of independence was delayed only by a lack of instructions from the various colonial assemblies.

JUNE 1776   Congress appoints a five-man committee to consider and prepare a Declaration of Independence.

The Declaration was mainly the work of Thomas Jefferson who wrote most of the document.

2 JULY 1776   Congress approves independence.

The Congress accepted the following resolution by Richard Henry Lee of Virginia: "That these United Colonies are, and of right ought to be, free and independent states, that they are absolved from all allegiance to the British Crown . . ."

4 JULY 1776   Congress approves the Declaration of Independence.

The document was signed by 55 delegates representing the thirteen states. The first signature is that of the President of Congress, John Hancock, who signed in such large letters so that, he said, "the King of England can read it without his glasses".

Independence was declared in each colony as a copy of the Declaration arrived there. In Georgia, this was not until mid-August.

DECLARATION OF INDEPENDENCE

In Congress 4th July, 1776.

The original draft of the Declaration of Independence, drawn up by Thomas Jefferson.

The Declaration of Independence:

When, in the course of human events, it becomes necessary for one people to dissolve the political bands which have connected them with another, and to assume among the powers of the earth, the separate and equal station to which the laws of nature and of nature's God entitle them, a decent respect to the opinions of mankind requires that they should declare the causes which impel them to the separation.

We hold these truths to be self-evident – that all men are created equal; that they are endowed by their Creator, with certain inalienable rights; that among these are life, liberty, and the pursuit of happiness. That to secure these rights, governments are instituted among men, deriving their just powers from the consent of the governed; that whenever any form of government becomes destructive of these ends, it is the right of the people to alter or to abolish it, and to institute new government, laying its foundation on such principles, and organizing its powers in such form, as to them shall seem most likely to effect their safety and happiness. Prudence, indeed, will dictate, that governments long established, should not be changed for light and transient causes; and, accordingly, all experience hath shewn that mankind are more disposed to suffer, while evils are sufferable, than to right themselves by abolishing the forms to which they are accustomed. But when a long train of abuses and usurpations, pursuing invariably the same object, evinces a design to reduce them under absolute despotism, it is their right, it is their duty, to throw off such government, and to provide new guards for their future security. Such has been the patient sufferance of these colonies, and such is now the necessity which constrains them to alter their former systems of government. The history of the present king of Great Britain, is a history of repeated injuries and usurpations, all having in direct object the establishment of an absolute tyranny over these states. . .

. . . We, therefore, the representatives of the United States of America, in general congress assembled, appealing to the Supreme Judge of the world for the rectitude of our intentions, do, in the name and by the authority of the good people of these colonies, solemnly publish and declare, that these United Colonies are, and of right ought to be, free and independent states – That they are absolved from all allegiance to the British crown, and that all political connection between them and the state of Great Britain is, and ought to be, totally dissolved; and that, as free and independent states, they have full power to levy war, conclude peace, contract alliances, establish commerce, and to do all other acts and things which independent states may of right do. And for the support of this declaration, with a firm reliance on the protection of Divine Providence we mutually pledge to each other our lives, our fortunes, and our sacred honor.

Lines 7-9 are the most famous and well-known lines of the Declaration. What do you think is meant by "all men are created equal"?

Do lines 9-15 justify the American Revolution?

Did lines 29-42 make war inevitable? Why?/Why not?

Who appears to be blamed for the troubles in the American colonies?

There was no formal declaration of war between the American colonies and Britain. There did not have to be. Some fighting had already taken place and the British were making plans to re-assert their authority in Boston. The Declaration of Independence made all-out war certain. The British had to fight to regain control of the thirteen colonies.

SEPTEMBER 1776 British occupy New York.
During August a large military force was sent from Britain to America, to fight under the command of Sir William Howe. Over 32,000 British troops and German mercenaries recruited for the American war were landed. They were joined by volunteers from Canada and other colonies which remained loyal to the Crown, as well as by loyalists from the thirteen colonies.
New York was taken by the British in September.

DECEMBER 1776 British occupy Rhode Island.
Washington's army retreats into Pennsylvania.
The Continental Army had been formed out of volunteers. Desertion was

QUEBEC

MAINE

MONTREAL

R. St. Lawrence

LAKE CHAMPLAIN

VERMONT

CROWN POINT

FORT TICONDEROGA

NEW HAMPSHIRE

FALMOUTH

PORTSMOUTH

Bennington 1777

Saratoga 1777 ✗

CONCORD

CHARLESTOWN

CAMBRIDGE

BOSTON

Bunker Hill 1775 ✗

LAKE ONTARIO

ALBANY

MASSACHUSETTS

Lexington 1775 ✗

NEW YORK

NEWPORT

RHODE ISLAND

NEW LONDON

WEST POINT

R. Hudson

CONNECTICUT

LONG ISLAND

MORRISTOWN

NEW YORK

BROOKLYN

PENNSYLVANIA

PRINCETON

Monmouth 1778 ✗

TRENTON

VALLEY FORGE

GERMANTOWN

PITTSBURG

Brandywine 1777 ✗

PHILADELPHIA

NEW JERSEY

MARYLAND

BALTIMORE

DELAWARE

ATLANTIC

OCEAN

Chesapeake Bay

RICHMOND

WILLIAMSBURG

Yorktown 1781 ✗

VIRGINIA

NORFOLK

Guilford Court House 1781 ✗

NORTH CAROLINA

Cowpens 1781 ✗

Waxhaws 1780 ✗

WILMINGTON

CAMDEN

SOUTH CAROLINA

CHARLESTON

SAVANNAH

GEORGIA

FLORIDA

TERRITORIES OCCUPIED OR CONTROLLED BY COLONISTS 1776

BY BRITISH

✗ BATTLES

Atlantic Ocean

Pacific Ocean

Battles of the American Revolution.

common, especially at harvest-time when men returned home to their land. In December 1776 the army had not yet been formed into an effective fighting force. The revolutionary militia or minute men were the other part of the rebel forces. They were part-time soldiers who remained at home but could be called out at short notice (in a "minute").

With the arrival of Howe and his large force Washington was forced to retreat.

A British Officer describes the American retreat:

As we go forward into the country, the rebels flee before us, and when we come back they always follow us, 'tis almost impossible to catch them. They will neither fight, nor totally run away, but they keep at such distance that we are always above a day's march from them. They seem to be playing at Bo-Peep.

(*Source:* letter from a British Officer, September 1776)

The British pursued Washington into New Jersey and to the Delaware river. Winter weather halted the British offensive and Washington tried to re-group his forces who were demoralized by retreat.

Rallying American troops, 1776:

Tom Paine, an English writer and supporter of the American Revolution, enlisted in the Continental Army in 1776. While serving as a soldier he wrote a series of pamphlets designed to maintain American morale.

These are the times that try men's souls: the summer soldier and the sunshine patriot will, in this crisis, shrink from the service of his country: but that he stands it now deserves the love and thanks of man and woman. Tyranny, like hell, is not easily conquered; yet we have this consolation with us, that the harder the conflict, the more glorious the triumph. What we obtain too cheap, we esteem too lightly.

(*Source: The Crisis*, Thomas Paine, December 1776)

26 DECEMBER 1776   Washington defeats German troops at Trenton.

In a surprise attack on Boxing Day Washington's troops defeated the totally unprepared German mercenaries who were still celebrating Christmas.

3 JANUARY 1777   Washington defeats British at Princeton.

A surprise attack by the Americans forced British forces to retreat. Washington's successes were treated by the Americans as major victories although they never threatened British military supremacy. After Princeton, Washington marched north to winter quarters at Morristown. The British wintered around New York.

British strategy, 1777:

General John Burgoyne was appointed by London to lead an expedition from Canada. His army would go south by Lake Champlain, Ticonderoga and Saratoga; Howe's army was to advance up the river Hudson; and a third British force under Lieutenant-Colonel Barry St Leger was to march from Lake Ontario. The three armies were to meet at Albany to launch a massive offensive against the Americans.

Delays in orders from the British War Office in London meant that Howe's army never participated in the plan. Instead, Howe led his army in an attack on Philadelphia.

JUNE 1777   Burgoyne's army marches south.

JULY 1777   Burgoyne takes Fort Ticonderoga and marches to Albany.

SEPTEMBER 1777   Howe defeats Washington at Brandywine and occupies Philadelphia.

OCTOBER 1777   Burgoyne surrenders at Saratoga.

St Leger's advance had been stopped by the Americans and Howe was in Philadelphia. Burgoyne's army was attacked at Saratoga by American forces commanded by Horatio Gates and joined by many militiamen.

A letter from General Gates:

The voice of fame, ere this reaches you, will tell how greatly fortunate we have been in this department. Burgoyne and his whole army have laid down their arms, and surrendered themselves to me and my Yankees. Thanks to the Giver of all victory for this triumphant success. I got here the night before last, and the army are now encamped upon the heights to the southward of this city. . . . If Old England is not by this letter taught humility, then she is an obstinate old slut, bent upon her ruin.

(*Source:* letter from General Gates to his wife three days after the British surrender, October 1777)

General Burgoyne surrenders to General Gates at Saratoga, October 1777.

Saratoga – a British failure:

It is not due to the good conduct of the Americans that the campaign in general has been terminated so happily, but by the faults of the British government in wishing General Burgoyne to traverse more than 200 leagues of country almost a desert to join forces with General Howe. . . . This plan might have seemed to be a good one in the cabinet in London, but appears miserable in the eyes of those who had an exact knowledge of the nature of the country.

(*Source:* Report from Colonel Louis de Portail, engineer in chief to Washington, October 1777)

Lord Chatham's reaction:

William Pitt became Lord Chatham in 1766.

No man thinks more highly than I of the virtue and valour of British troops; I know they can achieve anything except impossibilities; and the conquest of English America is an impossibility. . . . you may swell every expense and every effort still more extravagantly; pile and accumulate every assistance you can buy or borrow; traffic and barter with every little pitiful German prince that sells his subjects to the shambles of a foreign power; your efforts are forever vain and impotent doubly so from this mercenary aid on which you rely; for it irritates to an incurable resentment the minds of your enemies. To overrun them with the mercenary sons of rapine and plunder; devoting them and their possessions to the rapacity of hireling cruelty. If I were an American, as I am an Englishman, while a foreign troop was landed in my country, I never would lay down my arms, never – never – never!

(*Source:* from a speech in the House of Lords by Lord Chatham, November 1777)

DECEMBER 1777   The armies did not fight continuously: in the north the winter was too cold and troops hibernated in winter quarters; in the south the summer was too hot for campaigning and the troops were able to rest.

During the winter of 1777-78 Howe's troops wintered in Philadelphia. Washington's army camped at Valley Forge. The American army suffered shortages of food, clothing and equipment, and many deserted.

Poor food – hard lodging – cold weather – fatigue – nasty clothes – nasty cookery – vomit half my time – smoked out of my senses – the devil's in't – I can't endure it.

(*Source:* from the diary of a surgeon, Albigence Waldo, December 1777)

THINGS TO DO AND THINK ABOUT:

From what you have read so far do you think that the British or the Americans seem more likely to gain victory in the war? Why?

What were the major difficulties for the two armies?

FEBRUARY 1778   France signs Treaty of Alliance with the Americans.

Because of her defeat by Britain in the Seven Years War, France seemed a natural ally for the colonists. Since 1776 France had supplied American forces with munitions but was reluctant to become involved in direct conflict with Britain. The American rebels needed not only munitions but also French naval power to check British supremacy in the Atlantic. The British Navy supported the land forces by covering their positions on the coast, delivering supplies, transporting forces along the coastline and stopping colonial shipping.

In 1776 Congress had sent Benjamin Franklin to France to plead the rebels' cause. He had had some success: the King of France gave a secret subsidy of a million *livres* to the Americans; many Frenchmen, such as the Marquis de Lafayette, volunteered to serve in Washington's army and in 1777 French ports, including those in the West Indies, were open for refuge to American ships. However, it was not until the British defeat at Saratoga that France became convinced that Britain could be beaten.

Treaty of Alliance, 6 February 1778:

Article VIII   Neither of the two parties shall conclude either truce or peace with Great Britain without the formal consent of the other first obtained; and they mutually engage not to lay down their arms until the independence of the United States shall have been formally or tacitly assured . . .

APRIL 1778   ### The changing rebel army:

During the spring of 1778 Washington's forces were drilled by the German officer Baron von Steuben. He taught them tactics and the art of co-ordinated manoeuvring. Under his influence the camp at Valley Forge was transformed by better accommodation and sanitation.

George Washington (left), Commander-in-Chief of the American Continental Army, riding with the Marquis de Lafayette (centre) and Baron von Steuben, two of the foreign officers who trained and commanded American troops.

From amateur to professional fighters:

I was sometimes astonished when American baggage fell into our hands . . . to see how every wretched knapsack, in which were only a few shirts and a pair of torn breeches, would be filled with such military works as The Instructions of the King of Prussia to his Generals, Theilke's Field Engineer, the partisans Jenny and Grandmaison. . . . This was a true indication that the officers of this army studied the art of war while in camp, which was not the case with the opponents of the Americans, whose portmanteaux was rather filled with bags of hair powder, boxes of sweet smelling pomatum, cards (instead of maps), and then often, on top of all, novels or stage plays.

(*Source:* from the diary of John Ewald, a German soldier fighting for the British, spring 1778)

A British recognition of defeat:

We know that the Americans are and must be independent: and yet we will not treat them as such. If government itself retains the least idea of sovereignty, it has already gone too far for that; if it entertains the least hope of peace, it has not gone far enough; and every step we shall take to put the Americans back from independency, will convince them the more of the necessity of going forward.

(*Source:* from a speech in the House of Commons by Thomas Pownall, a Whig MP and a former Governor of Massachusetts, March 1778)

THINGS TO DO AND THINK ABOUT:

Why do you think that a Treaty of Alliance with France was so important to American rebels? Can you think of any arguments against such a treaty which would convince (a) the Americans, (b) the French?

Why did Thomas Pownall believe that British policy towards American independence should change?

JUNE 1778   British forces evacuate Philadelphia: Battle of Monmouth.
Sir Henry Clinton took command of British forces in Philadelphia in May 1778 and began to evacuate his men from that city so that they could march to New York. From there they would be dispersed to Halifax to meet American armies, and to the West Indies and Florida to meet the French. As the British marched towards New York their twelve-mile baggage train was attacked at Monmouth by Washington. The battle was the longest and hottest of the war — the temperature was over 100°F. It was also the last major battle in the north. Neither side gained ground. The British withdrew to New York and the Americans remained in New Jersey.

Molly Pitcher was so-called because she carried water in a pitcher to the troops. Here she is drawn taking her wounded husband's place at the guns, at the Battle of Monmouth, 1778.

Do you think that the picture of Mollie Pitcher was intended for an American or British audience? Why?

Is the picture reliable evidence on the Battle of Monmouth? Why?/Why not?

DECEMBER 1778 British occupy Georgia.

British troops sent from New York were joined by troops from East Florida. They recaptured Georgia for the British and reinstated the Royal Governor who had fled to London at the start of the Revolution.

JUNE 1779 Spain declares war on Britain.

Spain allied herself with France and so declared war on Britain. The terms of the Spanish-French treaty included a direct naval attack on England.

AUGUST 1779 French fleet in the English Channel threatens invasion of England. The attack fails.

DECEMBER 1779 **Washington needs supplies:**

[The army] has been five or six weeks past on half allowance and we have not more than three days bread at a third allowance on hand, nor anywhere within reach. . . . Our magazines are empty . . . unless some extraordinary and immediate exertions are made by the States from which we draw our supplies, there is every appearance that the army will infallibly disband in a fortnight.

(*Source:* letter from George Washington to governors of the states adjacent to his winter camp at Morristown, December 1779)

The war moves south:

Until 1778 there had been little fighting in the southern colonies. However, French involvement in the war meant that the British West Indies were under threat from the French Navy. The southern colonies became important as a base from which the British could wage war in the Caribbean. East Florida was securely British and Georgia had been re-taken; the next step for the British was to secure South Carolina for the Crown.

MAY 1780 British capture Charlestown, South Carolina.
This was the greatest American defeat of the war. Five thousand rebels surrendered.

A British soldier describes the American defeat at Charlestown:

General Leslie with the Royal English Fusiliers and Hessian Grenadiers and some Artillery took possession of the town and planted the British colours by the gate, on the ramparts, and [General] Lincoln limped out at the end of the most ragged rabble I ever beheld. . .
. . . They laid down their arms between their abatis and surrendered prisoners of war. . . . The militia, poor creatures, could not be prevailed upon to come out. They began to creep out of their holes the next day.
By the capitulation they are allowed to go home and plow the ground. There only they can be useful.

(*Source:* quoted in *The Fire of Liberty*, Esmond Wright, Hamish Hamilton, 1983)

AUGUST 1780 Rebels' defeat at Camden.
The Americans launched a counter-offensive in the south under Horatio Gates, but were defeated by the British under Lord Cornwallis.

An engraving published in London in November 1780. Count de Rochambeau commanded the French army in America after France entered the war in 1778. The cartoon is a ludicrous representation of Rochambeau and his troops. The general is standing on the right with an officer's spear and an exaggeratedly long pigtail. His troops, with a wide range of noses, carry knapsacks like large muffs.

What do you think is the nationality of the cartoonist (page 16)? Give a reason for your answer. What was the purpose of such a cartoon?

JANUARY 1781   **Washington's despair:**

The history of this war is a history of false hopes and temporary devices, instead of system and of economy. We have no magazines nor money to form them, and in little time we shall have no men if we had money to pay them. We have lived upon expedients till we can live no longer.

(*Source:* letter from George Washington, January 1781)

The British are defeated at Cowpens.

Nathanael Greene replaced Horatio Gates as commander of the American army in the south. He divided the army and placed one section under Daniel Morgan. At Cowpens in January 1781 Morgan outmanoeuvred the British, who lost in one hour one thousand men, either killed, captured or wounded, and many stores. Only twelve Americans were killed.

Morgan then marched to join Greene at Guildford Court House. Greene united the two sections of the army and marched on to North Carolina. Pursued by Lord Cornwallis and his men, the Americans covered one hundred miles in five days. Greene finally led his forces back to Guildford Court House.

Americans and British cross country, a popular rhyme:

Cornwallis led a country dance,
the like was never seen, Sir,
much retrograde and much advance,
and all with General Greene, Sir.

(*Source:* quoted in *The Fire of Liberty*)

MARCH 1781   British victory at Guildford Court House.

Greene withdrew American forces from Guildford Court House and Cornwallis claimed a British victory. The British had lost more men than the Americans and had to withdraw to the safety of the coast. Greene was able to retreat, re-form and begin attacking the British in Georgia and South Carolina.

The Battle of Guildford Court House:

The battle was fought at or near Guildford Court House. . . . The battle was long, obstinate and bloody. We were obliged to give up the ground and lost our artillery, but the enemy have been so soundly beaten that they dare not move towards us since the action. . .

. . . Except the ground and artillery they have gained no advantage. On the contrary, they are little short of being ruined. . . . Our army is in good spirits, but the militia are leaving us in great numbers to return home to kiss their wives and sweethearts.

(*Source:* letter from General Greene, March 1781)

AUGUST 1781   Cornwallis occupies Yorktown.

Cornwallis hoped to renew communications by sea with the British in New York and receive support from the British Navy. A French fleet sailed from the West Indies and blocked the entrance to Chesapeake Bay, defeating the British fleet. Washington and Rochambeau marched south and began the siege of Yorktown on 28 September. Cornwallis was unable to escape by land or sea.

British under siege at Yorktown:

My situation now becomes very critical. We dare not show a gun to their old batteries and I expect that their new ones will open tomorrow morning. . . . The safety of the place is . . . so precarious that I cannot recommend that the fleet and army should run great risk in endeavouring to save us.

(*Source:* letter from Cornwallis to Sir Henry Clinton, Commander-in-Chief of British Forces in America, October 1781)

19 OCTOBER 1781   ### The British surrender:

Brigadier Charles O'Hara surrendered the British forces to Washington as Cornwallis felt too ill to appear.

The surrender of Cornwallis to Washington at Yorktown, 19 October 1781.

I have the mortification to inform your Excellency that I have been forced to give up the posts of York and Gloucester, and to surrender the troops under my command, by capitulation on the 19th inst. as prisoners of war to the combined forces of America and France.

(*Source:* letter from Cornwallis to Sir Henry Clinton, 20 October 1781)

The play, sir, is over. Washington has given a dinner for British General O'Hara.

(*Source:* letter from Lafayette to a friend on the surrender at Yorktown, October 1781)

When British troops surrendered their arms at Yorktown Cornwallis asked his army band to play an old British nursery rhyme which had been popular in Britain during the Civil War of the seventeenth century.

If buttercups buzzed after the bee,
If boats were on land, churches on sea,
If ponies rode men and grass ate the cows,
And cats should be chased to holes by the mouse,
If the mamas sold their babies to the gypsies for half a crown;
Summer were spring and the t'other way round,
Then all the world would be upside down.

News of the surrender reached the British Prime Minister, Lord North on 25 November 1781. He is reported to have cried, "Oh God, it is all over."

Why do you think that Lafayette and Lord North thought the surrender of Yorktown marked the end of the war?

What made the surrender at Yorktown different from that at Saratoga?

Do you think that Cornwallis believed that the world had turned upside down?

In the same way as there had not been a declaration of war in 1776 there was no declaration of peace in 1781. Three thousand British troops remained in America: the British still controlled New York, Long Island, Charlestown and Georgia. During the winter of 1781-82 Washington stayed with his troops in their New Jersey winter quarters while Greene and his men marched to South Carolina and surrounded the British at Charlestown.

5 MARCH 1782   **The Commons urge the King to make peace:**

The House would consider as enemies to His Majesty, and to the Country, all those who should advise, or by any means attempt, the further prosecution of the war on the continent of North America, for the purpose of reducing the revolting Colonies to obedience by force.

(*Source:* motion agreed by the House of Commons, March 1782)

20 MARCH 1782   Lord North resigns. A Whig coalition under Lord Rockingham takes power.

APRIL 1782   Britain secures her possessions in the West Indies by defeating the French in the naval battle of the Saints.

JULY 1782   British evacuate Savannah.
Lord Rockingham dies and is succeeded by Lord Shelbourne.

NOVEMBER 1782	Preliminary Articles of Peace agreed in Paris.
DECEMBER 1782	British evacuate Charlestown.
FEBRUARY 1783	British and Americans declare the cessation of hostilities.
SEPTEMBER 1783	Treaty of Paris signed. The colonies have become States.
NOVEMBER 1783	Final evacuation of British troops from New York.
JUNE 1785	John Adams becomes the first Ambassador of the United States of America to Great Britain.

John Adams's speech to George III:

. . . The appointment of a Minister from the United States to your Majesty's Court will form an epoch in the history of England and of America. I think myself more fortunate than all my fellow citizens in having the distinguished honour to be the first to stand in your Majesty's royal presence in a diplomatic character, and shall esteem myself the happiest of men if I can be instrumental in recommending my country more and more to your Majesty's royal benevolence, and of restoring an entire esteem, confidence and affection; or in better words, the old good nature and the good old humour between people who, though separated by an ocean, and under different governments, have the same language, a similar religion and kindred blood.

The King's reply:

. . . I wish you, sir, to believe, and that it may be understood in America, that I have done nothing in the late contest, but what I thought myself indispensably bound to do by the duty which I owed to my people. I will be very frank with you. I was the last to consent to the separation; but the separation having been made, and having become inevitable, I have always said, as I say now, that I would be the first to meet the friendship of the United States as an independent Power. The moment I see such sentiments and language as yours prevail, and a disposition to give to this country the preference, that moment I shall say, let the circumstances of language, religion and blood have their natural and full effect.

THINGS TO DO AND THINK ABOUT:

How different would the experiences of British and American soldiers have been?

What do you think each side was fighting for?

The war lasted for almost eight years. Why do you think it lasted so long? Can you suggest any reasons for the British defeat and American success?

Filling in the Background: Politics

THE POLITICAL SCENE IN BRITAIN BEFORE 1766

PARLIAMENTARY MONARCHY

George III came to the throne in 1760, at the age of twenty-two. He was not an absolute ruler but ruled with Parliament: the House of Commons and the House of Lords. This parliamentary monarchy had been achieved only after a series of political crises in the seventeenth century.

The years of that century had been marked by a Civil War, beginning in 1642, between King and Parliament; the execution of the King, Charles I, and the establishment of a Republic in 1649 under the rule of Oliver Cromwell as Lord Protector; the restoration of the monarchy in 1660; and another revolution in 1688, known as the "Glorious Revolution". Parliament overthrew the King, James II, and invited William of Orange and his wife Mary to take his place. This revolution confirmed that the monarch ruled by permission of Parliament and not by any God-given right. British parliamentary monarchy was thus established. Parliament ruled the country. Ministers were appointed by the King but needed the support of Parliament to remain in office.

George III, painted by A. Ramsay, c. 1767.

PARLIAMENT

Britain was not a democracy in the eighteenth century. The right to vote was restricted to men, and usually to men who owned land. The franchise was different in different parts of the country. In the counties and towns or boroughs only men who had land worth about 40 shillings a year in taxes could vote. In some boroughs only the mayor and corporation voted; in others, holders of certain properties, or ratepayers. Parliament was dominated by aristocrats and the landed gentry. Despite the narrow franchise those with power believed that the franchise was varied enough to ensure that the interests of all citizens were represented.

Virtual representation:

There can be no doubt . . . that . . . the greatest part of the people of England are represented: among nine millions of whom there are eight which have no vote in electing members of Parliament. . . . A member of Parliament chosen for any borough represents not only the constituents and inhabitants of that particular place, but he represents . . . all the other commons of this land, and the inhabitants of all the colonies and dominions of Great Britain.

(*Source:* speech by Lord Mansfield in the House of Lords, 1766)

The House of Commons, 1742.

WHIGS AND TORIES

There were no political parties in the modern sense. Groups of individuals might act together on certain issues but these "friends" were not a tight-knit group with an agreed set of principles. Real party alignments began to take place only after about 1784.

Members of Parliament were usually known as Whigs or Tories according to their family background, friends and general political outlook. The names Whig and Tory originated in 1679 when debates had taken place in Parliament concerning the eventual successor to Charles II. Those who claimed the right to exclude the King's brother, James, Duke of York, from the throne were called Whigs; those who supported James in his hereditary right to the throne were called Tories. James succeeded to the throne in 1685. Tories came to be associated with the interests of the country gentry and the Anglican Church; Whigs with aristocratic, landowning families and the wealthy middle class.

The great Whig families had dominated Parliament since the beginning of the eighteenth century. George III distrusted the extent of their influence and brought in others, such as the Earl of Bute, to high office. In using his influence to secure the appointment of ministers he liked and trusted, George III offended the old ruling families.

Opposition to the King could be widespread and united, inside and outside Parliament, if it was believed that he was using too much influence and dominating weak ministers in order to control Parliament. Some discontent was evident inside Parliament in 1763 when Bute tried to levy a tax on cider. The Act gave inspectors the right to visit premises and to count the amount of cider produced. William Pitt, a leading Whig, opposed the Act on the grounds of liberty:

> The poorest man in his cottage may bid defiance to all the force of the Crown. It may be frail, its roof may shake; the wind may blow through it; the storms may enter, the rain may enter – but the King of England cannot enter; all his forces dare not cross the threshold of the ruined tenement.

(*Source:* speech by William Pitt in the House of Commons, 1763)

Who do you think was more powerful in the eighteenth century, King or Parliament? Why?

THE WILKES AFFAIR

Discontent with the King and his ministers was also evident outside Parliament and widely expressed during the case of John Wilkes.

John Wilkes was a Member of Parliament and founder of a paper called *The North Briton*. In Number 45 of this paper, in April 1763, he criticized the government, denouncing "ministerial despotism" and the "prostitution of the Crown". George III urged his ministers to take action. Wilkes was expelled by the Commons, arrested, released because of parliamentary privilege and then fled to France. He was re-elected to the Commons in 1768 and again expelled. Public protest and riots followed the exclusion of an elected Member of Parliament. Wilkes was seen as a defender of liberty against an oppressive King.

The whole affair stimulated political debate about the role of Crown and Parliament, about freedom of speech and about the nature of liberty. The ordinary English citizen was strongly against absolute rule. Liberty did not yet mean the freedom to vote or to form a trade union, but freedom from absolute monarchy, freedom from arbitrary arrest, and equality before the law.

John Wilkes, by William Hogarth, 1763.

The controversy surrounding Wilkes was to be important for America because it created sympathy for the cause of "liberty". Many opponents of the way the government dealt with Wilkes became supporters of the American cause.

The view of a London linen draper, 1768:

The persons who wish to enslave America, would, if it lay in their power, enslave us.

(*Source:* quoted in *The March of Folly*, Barbara Tuchman, Abacus, 1985)

Why would ordinary people, who could not vote, protest at the expulsion of John Wilkes from Parliament?

Why do you think that Wilkes was drawn as a comical figure?

THE POLITICAL SCENE IN AMERICA

In 1760 the thirteen colonies along the Atlantic were like different nations. They had been founded for different reasons, at different times, and were inhabited by people of many national origins, trades and churches. The colonies had been peopled by religious groups, such as the Quakers, by indentured servants, transported criminals, slaves and by those simply seeking a new life in a new country, such as skilled and unskilled labourers.

... each province has its own [characteristics], founded on the government, climate, mode of husbandry, customs and peculiarity of circumstances. Europeans ... become in the course of a few generations, not only Americans in general, but either Pennsylvanians, Virginians or provincials under some other name. Whoever traverses the continent must easily observe those strong differences, which will grow more evident in time. The inhabitants of Canada, Massachusetts, the middle provinces, the southern ones will be as different as their climates; their only points of unity will be those of religion and language.

(*Source: Letters from an American Farmer 1770-1775* by St Jean de Crevecoeur, 1782)

Each colony was separately governed and all colonies were subject to the Crown; the Board of Trade in London was responsible for the supervision of day-to-day affairs in each colony. Eight of the colonies employed agents to represent their views and interests in London. Benjamin Franklin, who played a leading role in the Revolution of 1776, was the London agent for Pennsylvania, Georgia, New Jersey and Massachusetts.

Each colony had a Governor, a Governor's Council and an elected Assembly. Eight of the colonies were directly responsible to the Crown and their Governor and officials were appointed in London. The corporation colonies (those set up by a trading company), such as Rhode Island and Connecticut, elected their own Governors. The proprietary colonies of Pennsylvania, Delaware and Maryland, which had been founded by grants of land to a ruling family, had their Governor chosen by that family.

The Governor of each colony nominated a Council to advise him and this acted as a supreme court of law for the colony. The Council membership was made up of local men of wealth and influence.

The local Assemblies were elected by male property owners. Throughout the colonies, one in four white males was eligible to vote; women, Jews, Catholics, blacks and indentured servants were excluded from voting. The Assemblies had limited powers as their main function was to represent public opinion on all matters concerning the colony. However, they were able to control the power of the Governor, to a certain extent, as each Assembly had to agree to the payment of their Governor's salary.

By 1760 many colonists had begun to compare the local Assembly, as the only representative body in the colony, to the House of Commons. Some foresaw a possible conflict between the Assemblies in America and Parliament in Britain.

Power of the Assemblies:

In Britain the American governments are considered as Corporations empowered to make by-laws, existing only during the pleasure of Parliament. . . . In America they claim to be perfect States, not otherwise dependent on Great Britain than by having the same King.

(*Source:* letter from Governor Barnard of Massachusetts to Lord Barrington, Secretary for War in London, 1765)

Benjamin Franklin, 1783. From 1757 to 1775 Franklin was an American agent in Britain, explaining the colonial point of view to Members of Parliament.

America's view of Britain:

In 1766 Benjamin Franklin was asked by the House of Commons about "the temper of America towards Great Britain before the year 1763". He replied that the colonists

submitted willingly to the government of the Crown, and paid in all their courts, obedience to acts of Parliament. Numerous as the people are in the several old provinces, they cost you nothing in forts, citadels, garrisons or armies, to keep them in subjection. They were governed by this country at the expense only of a little pen, ink, and paper. They had not only a respect, but an affection, for Great Britain, for its laws, its customs and manners, and even a fondness for its fashions, that greatly increased the commerce. Natives of England were always treated with particular regard, to be an Old-England man was, of itself, a character of some respect, and gave a kind of rank among us.

(*Source:* "Examination of Benjamin Franklin in the House of Commons", 13 February 1766, quoted in J.P. Greene (ed.), *Colonies to Nation: 1763-1789*, New York, 1967)

THINGS TO DO AND THINK ABOUT:

Why did the colonists have not only a respect, but an affection for Britain?

Can you explain the difference between a Colonial Assembly and the House of Commons?

Filling in the Background: The British Empire

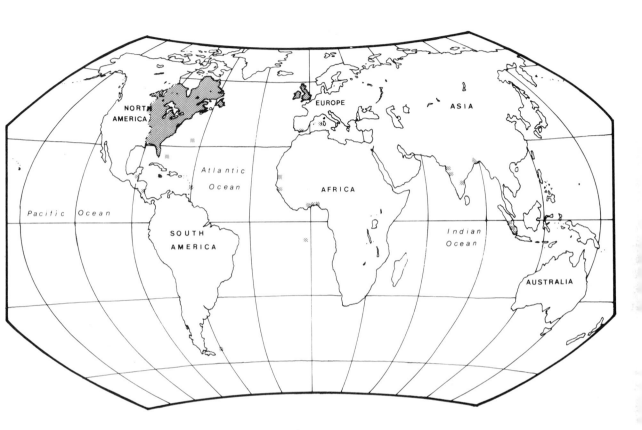

The British Empire in 1763.

The British Empire of the eighteenth century consisted of a number of trading stations, settlements and plantations in four main areas of the world: Africa, India, the West Indies and North America. The Empire was founded on trade, which was the basis of Britain's wealth and power. Trading stations had come into existence at the end of the sixteenth century when it was usual for a chartered company to be given royal permission to have sole trading rights in a particular area. This network of overseas possessions enabled Britain to supply her own needs in a range of raw materials and to maintain her shipping fleet.

The Africa Company, founded in 1588, had forts in Gambia and the Gold Coast and traded in gold, ivory, dyes and slaves. The East India Company, founded in 1600, had settlements along the Indian coast at Surat, Bombay and Madras, and these collected and distributed coffee from Arabia, silk from Persia, cotton and indigo from India, tea from China and spices from the East Indies. In 1606 the Virginia Company was formed and the first successful American settlement was made at Jamestown, Virginia in 1607. From the West Indies and the growing southern colonies like Virginia and the Carolinas, Britain received tobacco, rice, tar, sugar and some cotton. Those colonies in the north of America, which had a climate similar to that of Britain, provided little that could not be grown or made in England. These colonies were expected to provide markets for British goods.

The importance of trade:

The importance that Britain attached to trade in her Empire was emphasized by William Pitt when a young politician:

> When trade policy is at stake it is your last retrenchment. You must defend it or perish. (1739)

THE NAVIGATION ACTS

The pattern of trade within the Empire was governed by what became known as the Navigation Acts. These were a series of acts passed in 1651 and later, by governments determined to protect Britain's investment in her colonies. The Navigation Act required that all trade in the British Empire should be carried in British ships. The Enumerating Act listed articles which could not be exported from the colonies to foreign markets. (In 1722 these included ginger, sugar, wool, naval stores, cotton and tobacco.) The Staple Act prevented the import into the British colonies of nearly all goods direct from Europe.

A further series of acts restricted the development in the colonies of manufacturing industries which might compete with those in Britain, for instance, woollen and iron industries.

The ideal colony:

According to one contemporary observer, John Campbell, the ideal colony for Britain was one where

> the inhabitants wear not a rag of their own manufacturing; drive not a nail of their own forging; eat not out of a platter or mug of their own making.
>
> (*Source:* John Campbell, 1772, quoted in *The American War of Independence* by Peter Wells, Hodder, 1967)

In 1696 the Board of Trade and Plantations was established to administer all colonies from London, and in the interests of Britain. The Board continued to be responsible for the colonies until 1768, when a Secretary for the Colonies was appointed.

SLAVERY

Slavery was important in the Empire. British manufacturers and the East India Company produced goods to trade with African dealers for slaves. Slaves were transported from West Africa to the Caribbean to work on sugar plantations, and to the southern colonies of America to work on tobacco and rice plantations. Sugar was sent in refined form to Britain, and in the form of molasses to the northern American colonies, to be made into rum. The American colonies also sold food produce to the sugar-producing islands of the West Indies. There were black slaves throughout the American colonies but the majority were in the southern states of Virginia, Maryland and the Carolinas. In 1765 66% of the population of South

Carolina consisted of black slaves. Slavery was an integral part of the social and economic system of the southern colonies where a man's social status was determined by his ownership of land and slaves. In the northern colonies status was determined by wealth, which was often gained by trade.

THE AMERICAN COLONIES

To those in authority and with money in Britain the Empire was important. Politically, it guaranteed Britain's role as a world power, giving her much influence and prestige. Financially, the colonies, especially those in America, were a good investment and thriving market places.

The Imperial system was not unfavourable to the American colonies. American tobacco was the only tobacco allowed to be sold in Britain and tobacco growers in Gloucester were driven out of business so that there would be no British competition for American growers. The shipbuilding industry of the northern colonies thrived because of the need for shipping in colonial trade.

A colonist's approval of the Navigation Acts:

James Otis, the Attorney-General of Massachusetts and a leading revolutionary in 1776, approved of the Acts in 1764:

The act of navigation is a good act, so are all that exclude foreign manufacturers from the plantation, and every honest man will readily subscribe to them.

In the years immediately before the Revolution the colonists and the British tried to modify the old system of Empire. The British attempted to assert their rights to raise revenue by taxation in America; the Americans denied that right and wanted greater freedom in the Empire. While some colonists increasingly felt themselves to be equal partners in the Empire, they still acknowledged their duty to the King. Most Americans saw no alternative to the Imperial system.

Parts of a whole:

The Parliament unquestionably possesses a legal authority to regulate the trade of Great Britain and all her colonies. . . . We are but parts of a whole, and therefore there must exist a power somewhere to preside, and preserve the connection in due order. This power is lodged in the Parliament, and we are as much dependent on Great Britain as a perfectly free people can be on another. . .

(*Source: Letters from a Farmer in Pennsylvania* by John Dickinson. These appeared in the *Pennsylvania Gazette* between December 1767 and February 1768)

Even as late as 1775 men who were to be important revolutionary leaders were still prepared to remain in the British Empire.

A new role in the Empire:

We are a part of the British Dominions, that is of the King of Great

Britain, and it is our interest and duty to continue subject to the authority of Parliament in the regulation of our trade, as long as she shall leave us to govern our internal policy and to give and grant our own money, and no longer.

(*Source:* letter from John Adams, Massachusetts delegate to the 1st and 2nd Congresses, to Benjamin Franklin, January 1775)

John Adams, 1783, an engraving from a painting by J.S. Copley.

THINGS TO DO AND THINK ABOUT:

Why has the slave trade been called the triangular trade of the Empire? What arguments can you give for and against the Navigation Acts, from the point of view of (1) a British manufacturer, (2) an American?

Can you find anything in the extract from John Adams's letter with which the British might disagree?

Filling in the Background: Ideology

We know what happened after the war of independence; an independent republican state was established, called the United States of America. The revolutionaries of 1776 could not foresee the outcome of their actions. Their Declaration of Independence was a rejection of the colonies' past and of the British Empire, but also a step into an unknown future. The revolutionaries needed a philosophy to justify their revolt and to give them a vision of their new society.

A revolution is not possible without ideas; revolutionary leaders need a vision of what they might achieve. This is not to say that revolutions are planned and organized around a set of ideas, but their influence cannot be disregarded. Ideas are understood at different levels; people use them in their own way, perhaps to justify actions already taken or as a spur to action. The ideas looked at in this chapter were as available in Britain as they were in America. Ideas are used by those who need them, and Americans chose from British and American thought only those they needed.

REPUBLICANISM

The most important ideological influence on the American Revolution was republicanism: the belief that a state should be arranged so that the supreme power rests in the people and their elected representatives, rather than that the state should be governed by a monarch. There was no republican party in the colonies in the first part of the eighteenth century and none was formed until the late 1790s. Once the British monarchy was rejected, rebels were confronted by the reality of a state without a crowned head. Republicanism seemed the only answer.

The thinkers who most influenced the American revolutionaries were those of the seventeenth century in England who had experienced Civil War and the English Republic (1649-60). These were, for instance, John Milton and Algernon Sydney. John Milton had defended the execution of Charles I, arguing that people were born free and set up governments to protect them; the King had power only for the public good and if the King stopped working for the good of the people it was lawful to dispose of him.

The power of Kings:

The power of Kings and magistrates is nothing else, but what is only derivative, transferred and committed to them in trust from the people, to the common good of them all, in whom the power remains . . . and cannot be taken from them, without a violation of their natural birthright.

(*Source: Tenure of Kings and Magistrates*, John Milton, 1649)

After the restoration of the monarchy in 1660 the publication of republican sentiments was dangerous. Sydney was executed in 1683 and among the charges brought against him was that in his papers, such as *The Natural Power of Kings* in 1680, he had claimed that the King was not only subject to the law but also responsible to the people.

Republicans also believed that all men had natural rights such as freedom of speech and freedom from arbitrary arrest. They argued that government was based on law which protected liberty, and not on the whims of an absolute ruler.

JOHN LOCKE   John Locke's *Two Treatises of Government*, published in 1690, was an attempt to justify the Glorious Revolution of 1688. He argued that government was only possible because the people agreed to it and so, if the government betrayed its trust, it may be overthrown.

The people and obedience to the rulers:

Whenever the legislators endeavour to take away and destroy the property of the people, or to reduce them to slavery under arbitrary power, they put themselves into a state of war with the people, who are absolved from any further obedience . . .

(*Source:* John Locke, *The Second Treatise of Government*, 1690)

People and power:

. . . when by the miscarriages of those in authority [power] is forfeited . . . it reverts to the society and the people have a right to act as supreme, and continue the legislative in themselves; or erect a new form.

(*Source:* John Locke, *The Second Treatise of Government*, 1690)

American colonists claimed the liberties, rights and privileges of native-born English men and women in their quarrel with Parliament. In quoting John Locke, Americans were claiming the rights that had been established for the English in 1688.

American rights:

An American journalist wrote in 1764:

Whether you are Englishmen, Germans, Low-German or Swedes, whether you are of the High Church, Presbyterians, Quakers or of another denomination, by your living here and by the law of the land you are free men, not slaves. You have a right to all liberties of a native born Englishman and you have a share in the fundamental laws of the land.

(*Source:* Christopher Sower Jr., 1764)

Locke was quoted in many articles published in the colonies before 1776 and many Americans called him the "father of the Revolution".

An opposing view:

While many Americans quoted Locke on the rights of the people, Sir William Blackstone's *Commentaries on the Laws of England*, first published in London in 1765, provided an opposing view for those who wished to declare it. Blackstone proclaimed the unbounded legal authority of the Crown and Parliament. He disagreed with Locke that the people had a right to remove their rulers, if there were disagreements between them. He argued that only Parliament could make changes in Parliament:

So long as the English constitution lasts, . . . the power of Parliament is absolute and without control.

(*Source: Commentaries on the Laws of England*, Sir William Blackstone, 1774)

Americans might have preferred Locke but they could not ignore Blackstone whose *Commentaries* became the standard text in legal affairs on both sides of the Atlantic and was used as a reference book by both Continental Congresses.

THINGS TO DO AND THINK ABOUT:

When the thinkers quoted in this chapter use the term "the people", whom do they really mean and whom are they leaving out?

Do you think that members of the House of Commons would agree with the ideas of Locke and Milton? Why?/Why not?

Why were seventeenth-century thinkers important to eighteenth-century Americans?

THE ENLIGHTENMENT

The eighteenth century saw dramatic changes in the educated world; old ways of looking at society were challenged by new ideas in the arts, science, philosophy and religion in Europe. The changing view of the world became known as the Enlightenment. The thinkers of the Enlightenment, such as Rousseau, Diderot and Voltaire, questioned everything that had been accepted for centuries about society, religion and government. Enlightened thinkers believed that what was traditional was not necessarily good and that all institutions should be questioned and re-evaluated. They had a basic belief in the power of all human beings to understand and change the world, because improvement was possible. American colonists who questioned their relationship with the Crown were in the tradition of the Enlightenment.

The colonies and the Enlightenment:

In 1955 an American historian and a British historian collaborated on a history of the United States of America. In their book, *The Birth of the U.S.A.*, they wrote the following about the colonies and the Enlightenment:

The United States itself . . . emerged at a time when the western world was shifting from one system of thought to another, each involving quite different views of man, the world, and the Deity beyond them. The

American colonies were children of . . . the Enlightenment. John Locke . . . wrote a charter for the Carolinas; Rousseau and Franklin were friends . . . Voltaire was still living when the Continental Congress signed the Declaration of Independence. The Enlightenment . . . provided the first nationalized pattern of American thought. There was an American Enlightenment but it was late . . . and singularly American. Eighteenth century America was not merely an extension or a reflection of contemporary Britain or Europe . . . there was a culture lag in the transmission of patterns of thinking from one side of the Atlantic to the other.

. . . Americans chose from British and European thought only those ideas they needed or those in which they had a special interest . . . The Americans bent the Enlightenment to American uses.

(*Source: A History of the U.S.A. 1. The Birth of the U.S.A.*, R.B. Nye and J.E. Morpurgo, Penguin, 1970)

THINGS TO DO AND THINK ABOUT:

America in the eighteenth century was still a "new world". Do you think that new ideas have a better chance of success in such a world? Why?/Why not?

Look again at the Declaration of Independence. Do you think that it was influenced by any of the ideas mentioned in this chapter?

The Beginning of Colonial Discontent: From the Seven Years War to the First American Congress

1763 End of the Seven Years War and the Peace of Paris.

1763 marked the end of the Seven Years War in which Britain had fought against France in India, Africa, the West Indies and Canada. The war had been fought by Imperial powers in their rivalry for Empire. In the Peace of Paris which ended the war Britain took control of Canada, Florida, the West Indian islands of Grenada, Dominica, St Vincent and Tobago, and Senegal in Africa.

British success in the war brought economic problems: there was a post-war slump, massive deficits, and the war had doubled the national debt. The cost of defending and administering Britain's growing Empire was crippling and increasing.

TAXATION The newly appointed Prime Minister, George Grenville, had to make decisions about how to raise money to pay for the defence and administration of the American colonies. Money could be raised by taxation, but the controversial questions were: What duties could be levied? and Who would pay them?

The main tax in Britain was the land tax, which produced almost a quarter of the government's revenue. The remainder came from customs duties paid on the export and import of goods; the excise, a charge made on goods during their manufacture or before their sale; stamp duty, a general tax on printed matter such as newspapers and legal documents; and indirect taxation on a range of goods.

In 1763 the Americans paid no direct taxes to Parliament. A small amount of tax was raised in each colony by the Governor and the Assembly for local matters. The Americans were not used to paying taxes. They were used only to Parliament regulating colonial trade and imposing customs duties.

MARCH 1764 **Sugar Act:**

The Sugar Act was the first piece of legislation designed to raise revenue in the colonies. The government made clear that the intention of the Act was to "raise a revenue in America for defraying the expenses of defending, protecting and securing the same". The Act dealt mainly with the importation into the colonies of sugar and its by-products, molasses and rum, from the West Indies. To protect British West Indian sugar planters from competition from planters in the French West Indies, the molasses duty was lowered; the import of rum was forbidden; and the sugar duty was raised for imports from foreign territories. American merchants routinely resorted to smuggling to avoid British trade regulations and so the Sugar Act also attempted to strengthen the customs service and make the regulations effective.

Britain was asserting her right to tax her subjects in the colonies, but the colonists, who had never been taxed by Britain, denied that Parliament had such a right. Colonial agents in London protested and petitions were sent from America. On both sides of the Atlantic it was pointed out that Britain earned more from trade with America than she could ever do from taxation, and that trade might suffer if unpopular legislation were enforced.

The full effect of the Sugar Act had not been assessed by the time Parliament began debating the imposition of a new tax on the colonies – stamp duty.

FEBRUARY 1765   **Parliament debates the taxation of the colonies:**

By February 1765 the members of the House of Commons were aware of colonial resentment and indignation at the proposed Stamp Act. Petitions had arrived from the colonies opposing the Act and reports of colonial opposition were being published in London newspapers.

Shall the Americans . . . children planted by our Arms, shall they grudge to contribute their mite to relieve us from the heavy weight of that burden we lie under?

(*Source:* speech in the House of Commons, February 1765, by Charles Townsend, President of the Board of Trade)

They planted by your care? No! Your oppressions planted them in America. . . . They nourished by your indulgence? They grew up by your neglect of them. . . . They protected by your arms? They have nobly taken up arms in your defence. . . . And believe me, and remember that I this day told you so, that same spirit of freedom which actuated that people at first will accompany them still. . . . They are a people jealous of their liberties and who will vindicate them if they should be violated.

(*Source:* speech in the House of Commons, February 1765, by Colonel Isaac Barre, an MP who had fought in Canada against the French in the Seven Years War)

MARCH 1765   The Stamp Act is passed.

The Stamp Act required that stamp duties be paid in the American colonies on all printed matter: legal documents, pamphlets, newspapers, playing cards and dice. Stamps had to be bought by the customer to legalize the documents, and duties ranged from one halfpenny to £10. The duty was payable in coins, not notes. Americans were appointed as stamp masters to administer the new tax.

Compared with opposition to the Sugar Act, opposition to the Stamp Act was much more widespread in the colonies because its provisions affected a far larger range of the community: inn-keepers, merchants, newspaper men and lawyers.

MAY 1765   Local Assemblies protest.

The Virginian Assembly passed a set of anti-stamp resolutions. These were introduced by Patrick Henry, who ten years later was to call for armed resistance to Britain and become one of the leaders of the Revolution. Henry argued that the colonists were free to tax themselves and would accept taxation imposed by their elected representatives. Taxes could not be levied by Parliament, for it did not have representatives from the colonies. The famous cry of "No taxation without representation!" arose out of Henry's speech.

Resolutions of the Virginian Assembly:

Resolved, That the taxation of the people by themselves or by persons chosen by themselves to represent them, who can only know what taxes the people are able to bear, or the easiest method of raising them, and must themselves be affected by every tax laid on the people, is the only security against a burthensome taxation, and the distinguishing characteristick of British freedom, without which the ancient constitution cannot exist.

(*Source:* part of resolutions by the Virginian Assembly, May 1765)

Patrick Henry went even further in condemning the Stamp Act and warned:

Caesar had his Brutus, Charles I his Cromwell, and George III may profit by their example . . . if this be treason make the most of it.

(*Source:* Patrick Henry in the Virginian Assembly, May 1765)

The front page of an American newspaper protesting against the Stamp Act. It claims that the duty will bring about the paper's death.

The Virginian Governor dissolved the Assembly the day after Henry's speeches.

7-25 OCTOBER 1765	**Stamp Act Congress:**

Delegates from nine of the original British colonies met in New York to discuss opposition to the Stamp Act. New Hampshire, Virginia, North Carolina and Georgia declined to send delegates. The Congress organized a boycott of British goods by urging that Americans should not buy British goods until the Stamp Act was repealed. The boycott was known as Non-importation and, throughout the thirteen colonies, merchants agreed to stop trading with Britain.

NOVEMBER 1765	Rioting in protest at the Stamp Act.

American popular feeling was expressed in many ways. Stamp agents were burned in effigy and their houses were set on fire. By November, when the Act should have become operative, all the stamp agents had resigned because of intimidation.

An American cartoon celebrating the repeal of the Stamp Act.

Everything that for years past had been the cause of any popular discontent was revived and private resentments against people in office worked themselves in and endeavoured to execute themselves under the mask of the public cause.

(*Source:* Governor Barnard of Massachusetts to the Earl of Halifax, November 1765)

MARCH 1766	Parliament repeals the Stamp Act and passes the Declaratory Act.

The Declaratory Act:

[Parliament] . . . hath, and of right ought to have full power and authority to make laws and statutes of sufficient force and validity to bind the colonies and people of America, subjects of the Crown of Great Britain, in all cases whatsoever.

(*Source:* from the Declaratory Act, 1766)

THINGS TO DO AND THINK ABOUT:

Why would the British government find the argument of "no taxation without representation" unacceptable?

Why did the Americans question the right of Parliament to impose taxes on them?

If the government was prepared to repeal the Stamp Act why was the Declaratory Act passed?

Can you suggest alternative ways of raising money to those followed by the British government?

JUNE 1767 Further duties are imposed on the colonies.
  Charles Townsend, Chancellor of the Exchequer, imposed a series of duties on goods imported into the American colonies. These included duties on tea, glass, lead, paint and paper. The Townsend Acts also put an end to the colonial Assemblies' control of Governors' salaries. British Governors and judges were to be paid out of customs duties collected by British revenue officers.

FEBRUARY 1768 **The Massachusetts Letter:**

The Massachusetts Assembly wrote to other Assemblies in the colonies asking them to co-ordinate resistance to the Townsend duties. Only Pennsylvania refused to join an alliance of the colonies against British taxation.

OCTOBER 1768 British troops sent to Boston.
  British officials were increasingly concerned at American opposition to the Townsend duties. Troops were sent to Boston to reinforce several British garrisons in the colonies. Boston was reinforced by four regiments.

NON-IMPORTATION ND THE EFFECT ON BRITISH TRADE By the autumn of 1769 all colonies except New Hampshire had adopted non-importation agreements in their Assemblies. Generally, they agreed to boycott luxury goods such as spirits, sugar, pewter, hats and shoes. From 1768 to 1769 English exports to America dropped by a third, from approximately £2,400,000 to £1,600,000. New York cut its imports to one-seventh of what they had been in 1764: from £482,000 in 1764 to £74,000 in 1769.

Receipts from the Townsend duties in their first year amounted to £16,000. Compare this with military expenditure for America of £170,000.

JANUARY 1770   Lord North becomes Prime Minister.

MARCH 1770   **The Boston Massacre:**

On 5 March a mob began to taunt a British sentry on duty outside a Customs House in Boston. The mob shouted abuse at the soldier and threw snow and ice at him. Six privates, a corporal and the officer of the day, Captain Preston, appeared from the guardhouse and in the crowd of soldiers and the mob five shots were fired. Five Americans were killed as a result of the gun fire. The soldiers were tried by a local jury: two were found guilty of manslaughter and the rest were acquitted. This so-called "Boston Massacre" was publicized in inflammatory broadsides and prints across the thirteen colonies. The prints, of which there were several

The Boston Massacre, from an engraving by Paul Revere.

versions, were pieces of propaganda against British rule. They were inaccurate. The soldiers did not line up to fire on innocent citizens. What was most important was what Americans convinced themselves must have happened.

APRIL 1770 Townsend duties abolished.

Townsend died in September 1767. Lord North believed that the duties were not achieving anything worthwhile and abolished them, but left the tax on tea as an expression of parliamentary rights. American merchants simply smuggled in tea to avoid paying the duty and in 1771 ninety per cent of the tea drunk in the colonies was thought to have been smuggled.

JUNE 1772 ## The *Gaspee* incident:

The *Gaspee* was a British customs ship which attempted to catch smugglers. It ran aground off Rhode Island and local merchants organized enough men to attack the ship, put the crew ashore and then burned it. The British authorities declared that the burning of the ship was an act of war, set up an investigatory commission and declared that the culprits would be sent to England for trial. No-one informed on the culprits and the matter could not be pursued.

SPRING 1773 Committees of Correspondence formed.

The colonies agreed to the proposal from the Virginian Assembly that a chain of inter-colonial Committees of Correspondence should be set up, so that there would be joint action against acts of oppression.

THINGS TO DO AND THINK ABOUT:

How do you think the Boston Massacre and the Gaspee *incident were used by American rebels?*

All of the soldiers involved in the Boston Massacre were acquitted of murder. Would this have changed popular feeling?

MAY 1773 Tea Act passed by Parliament.

In 1773 the British East India Company was in serious financial difficulties. Bankruptcy for the company would have been a disaster for the funds of the British government, which had a great deal invested in it. The Tea Act was one of the measures the government used to rescue the British East India Company. It allowed tea to be imported directly to the American colonies from India, so cutting the costs of the middlemen in England. The price of East India Company tea in America would be lower even than that of smuggled tea. The Indian tea was to be sent to a selected group of merchants for distribution, thus giving them a monopoly.

The Sons of Liberty:

The Sons of Liberty had first been formed in Connecticut in 1765. Groups of men organized themselves to coordinate effective attacks on people and property representing British rule in the colonies. It was a loose organization: in some areas the names of members were kept secret and in others they were not. The Sons of Liberty and Daughters of Liberty were successful in enforcing the boycott of British goods.

When the tea ships from India arrived in New York, some citizens formed a group of the Sons of Liberty to organize opposition to the landing of the tea.

New York Sons of Liberty Resolution on Tea, November 1773:

... To prevent a calamity which, of all others, is the most to be dreaded – slavery ... we, subscribers being influenced from a regard to liberty .. . agree to associate together under the name and style of the 'sons of liberty of New York' and engage our honor to, and with each other, faithfully to observe and perform the following resolutions.

1st. Resolved.   That whoever shall aid or abet, or in any manner assist in the introduction of tea, from any place whatsoever, into this colony, while it is subject, by a British act of Parliament, to the payment of a duty, for the purpose of raising a revenue in America, he shall be deemed an enemy to the liberties of America.

2nd. Resolved.   That whoever shall be aiding, or assisting, in the landing, or carting, of such tea, from any ship or vessel, or shall hire any house, store-house, or cellar or any place whatsoever to deposit the tea, subject to a duty as aforesaid, he shall be deemed an enemy to the liberties of America.

The British East India Company did not sell any tea in the colonies. Mob violence and the resignation of those who were supposed to receive and sell the tea meant that the tea ships were turned back from New York and Philadelphia. Tea was landed at Charlestown but kept in a warehouse. In Boston, Massachusetts, the tea ships docked but were prevented from unloading their cargoes.

DECEMBER 1773   **The Boston Tea Party:**

Boston Sons of Liberty boarded the tea ships and threw 342 chests of tea overboard.

Dressed for the Party:

It was now evening, and I immediately dressed myself in the costume of an Indian, equipped with a small hatchet, which I and my associates denominated the tomahawk, with which, and a club, after having painted my face and hands with a coal dust in the shop of a blacksmith, I repaired to Griffin's Wharf, where the ships lay that contained the tea. When I first appeared in the street after being thus disguised, I fell in with many who were dressed, equipped and painted as I was, and who fell in with me and marched in order to the place of our destination. . . . We then were ordered by our commander to open the hatches and take out all the chests

The Boston Tea Party. of tea and throw them overboard, and we immediately proceeded to execute his orders, first cutting and splitting the chests with our tomahawks, so as thoroughly to expose them to the effects of the water . . .

(*Source:* an account by George Hewes, 1773)

MARCH-JUNE 1774

Intolerable or Coercive Acts passed, a series of Acts designed to punish Boston for its tea party:
1. Boston Port Act: the port of Boston was closed to all trade until the losses of the East India Company had been paid.
2. Massachusetts Government Act: all local government was taken over by a newly appointed military Governor. General Thomas Gage combined the role of military Governor of Massachusetts with his existing one of Commander-in-Chief of British forces in America.
3. Justice Act, called by Americans "the Murder Act": any British official or officer in Massachusetts accused of a capital offence could be tried in Britain.
4. Quartering Act (this Act applied in every colony): troops could be billeted away from barracks in local properties. This gave the military freedom of movement within the colonies.

Why were these Acts "intolerable"?

Why were they known in England as "coercive" rather than "intolerable"?

What does the cartoonist (see overleaf) think of the Acts?

"The able Doctor, or America Swallowing the Bitter Draught", an engraving from the London Magazine, *1774. The print illustrated a report on the debate of the Boston Port Bill. America is held down by Lord Mansfield, Lord Chief Justice, while Lord North pours tea down her throat and America spews it back. In Lord North's pocket is a copy of the Boston Port Bill. Lord Sandwich, First Lord of the Admiralty, holds America's legs. Behind Mansfield stands a shocked Britannia and Lord Bute with a sword engraved "Military Law". On the left are the figures of France and Spain.*

APRIL 1774

Government's American policy criticized in the Commons:

Edmund Burke, a Whig who opposed the government's policies in America, argued that present policies would lead to ruin.

Never . . . have the servants of the state looked at the whole of your complicated interests in one connected view. . . . They never had any system of right or wrong but only invented occasionally some miserable tale for the day in order meanly to sneak out of difficulties into which they had proudly strutted. . . . By such management . . . they have shaken the pillars of commercial Empire. . . . They tell you that your dignity is tied to it. . . . This dignity is a terrible encumbrance to you for it has of late been ever at war with your interests.

(*Source:* speech by Edmund Burke in the House of Commons, 19 April 1774)

SEPTEMBER 1774

First Continental Congress meets in Philadelphia:

The Massachusetts Assembly, which now met unofficially, suggested that a Congress of all the colonies should be held to discuss opposition to British policies in America. Twelve states took part and were represented by 56 delegates; Georgia did not attend. The Congress met for six weeks

to consult on the present state of the Colonies . . . and determine upon wise and proper measures . . . for the recovery of their just rights and liberties . . . and the restoration of union and harmony between Great Britain and the Colonies.

Before dispersing, the Congress agreed to set up a Continental Association across the colonies. The Association was to impose a new boycott on British goods and discourage exports to Britain.

Local committees were zealous in their duties and people who wore English hats or drank tea were likely to be named and condemned in local newspapers. In some cases people were tarred and feathered as a punishment for ignoring the boycott.

A loyalist American pleads:

If I must be enslaved, let it be by a King at least, and not by a parcel of upstart lawless Committee-men. If I must be devoured, let me be devoured by the jaws of a lion, and not gnawed to death by rats and vermin.

(*Source:* writings of the Reverend Samuel Seabury, New York, 1774)

"A New Method of Macarony Making, as practised at Boston", a print published in London in October 1774. ("Macarony" was the eighteenth-century name for English dandies whose clothes exaggerated the heights of fashion.) The picture is based on an incident in January 1774, when the Commissioner for Customs in Boston, John Malcolm, was tarred and feathered, led to the gallows and forced to drink a great deal of tea. In the picture, the cockade on the hat on the right means that the man is one of the Sons of Liberty. The "45" on the other hat refers to the "number 45" of The North Briton *by John Wilkes. The suggestion is that tar and feathers were fashionable for Customs Officers in the colonies in 1774.*

Advice to Americans:

But, Oh! God bless our honest King
The Lords and Commons, true.
And if, next, Congress be the thing
Oh, bless that Congress, too!

(*Source:* "A Poor Man's Advice to his Poor Neighbors", a ballad, New York, 1774)

The King's View:

The die is now cast, the colonies must either submit or triumph; I do not wish to come to severer measures but we must not retreat.

(*Source:* letter from George III to Lord North, 11 September 1774)

NOVEMBER 1774   **The King writes to the Prime Minister, Lord North:**

... The New England governments are in a state of rebellion, blows must decide whether they are to be a subject to this country or independent.

(*Source:* letter from George III to Lord North, 18 November 1774)

I return the private letters received from Lieut-General Gage; his idea of suspending the Acts appears to me the most absurd that can be suggested. The people are ripe for mischief, upon which the mother-country adopts suspending the measures she has thought necessary: this must suggest to the colonies a fear that alone prompts them to their present violence; we must either master them or totally leave them to themselves and treat them as aliens.

(*Source:* letter from George III to Lord North, 19 November 1774)

THINGS TO DO AND THINK ABOUT:

Burke believed that the government was so concerned with keeping its dignity that it could not resolve its problems in America. From what you have read so far, do you think that could be true? How could the government have resolved the American crisis in April 1774?

What appears to have been the attitude of the King in 1774?

Not all colonists were as anti-British as the Sons of Liberty. What do the extracts from Seabury and the New York ballad tell you about other views in America?

JANUARY 1775   The Earl of Chatham proposed an immediate withdrawal of British troops from Boston. He urged conciliation with the colonists so that the Empire could be saved from war:

Let this distinction remain; taxation is theirs, commercial regulation is ours. As an American I would recognise to England her supreme right of regulating commerce and navigation: as an Englishman, I recognise to the Americans their supreme unalienable right in their property; a right which they are justified in the defence of . . . they will defend themselves, their families and their country.

(*Source:* speech in the House of Commons by Lord Chatham (Pitt), January 1775)

MARCH 1775 My hold of the colonies is in the close affection which grows from common names, from kindred blood, from similar privileges, and equal protection. These are ties, which though light as air, are as strong as links of iron. Let the colonies always keep the idea of their civil rights associated with your government; they will cling and grapple to you; and no force under heaven will be of power to tear them from their allegiance.

(*Source:* speech on Conciliation with America, by Edmund Burke, House of Commons, March 1775)

Burke's motion for conciliation with the colonies was heavily defeated in the House of Commons.

Later in March Lord North sent three regiments to New York to reinforce British troops in America; three generals went with them: Major-Generals William Howe, John Burgoyne and Henry Clinton.

What are Chatham's and Burke's criticisms of government policy?

Do you think that events would have been the same if different people had been in control in London?

THE SITUATION AT THE END OF MARCH 1775 By the end of March it appeared that only force of arms would settle the dispute between the colonies and Parliament. In all thirteen colonies military stores were being collected and volunteer armies were being organized. Royal Governors were finding it increasingly difficult to manage their colonies.

General Gage, the British Commander-in-Chief and Governor of Massachusetts since May 1774, was in an impossible position. The Massachusetts Assembly continued to meet although it had been banned, and it had gathered military supplies and companies of volunteers ready to turn out to fight at a moment's notice; these volunteers were often called "minutemen". The Secretary of State for the Colonies, Lord Dartmouth, urged Gage by letter from London to use force to support the Coercive Acts and to arrest leading rebels, as those Americans who no longer accepted British authority were called. Gage was reluctant to act as he did not have sufficient forces, despite some reinforcements from Canada. Gage's men numbered about 3,500 and he had asked London for 20,000.

The generals Burgoyne, Clinton and Howe, with some reinforcements of men and ships, did not leave Britain until April 1775.

Blows Must Decide

MARCH 1775

British rule denounced in Virginia.

The rebel Virginian Convention or Provincial Congress met in Richmond, Virginia. Some of its members still resisted the call for the Convention to recognize the various local volunteer forces as the Virginian Militia. Patrick Henry had no doubt that the time had come for armed resistance and one phrase from his speech to the Convention became the rallying cry for many rebels:

I know not what course others may take; but as for me give me liberty or give me death!

(*Source:* Patrick Henry, 23 March 1775)

18-19 APRIL 1775

Lexington and Concord: the first shots of the war:

General Gage ordered a force of 700 men from Boston to destroy rebel military supplies at Concord, New Hampshire. Warned of the British approach, local militia men organized and tried to halt the British, first at Lexington and then at Concord. At Lexington the British dispersed a small American force; then they marched on to Concord where they destroyed a small part of the rebel stores. The British return to Boston was made very difficult by the rebels and was accomplished only with the support of more troops sent out from there. The American rebels claimed victory and laid siege to Boston. Estimated casualties: American 95; British 272.

The British are coming!

We at Concord heard they was a-coming. The Bell rung at 3 o'clock for an alarm. As I was then a Minuteman, I was soon in town and found my captain and the rest of my company at the post. It wasn't long before there was other minute companies. One company, I believe, of minute-men was raised in almost every town to stand at a minute's warning. Before sunrise there was, I believe, 150 of us and more of all that was there. . .

When we was on the hill by the bridge, there was about eighty or ninety British came to the bridge and there made a halt. After a while they begun to tear up the plank off the bridge. Major Buttrick said if we were all of his mind, he would drive them away from the bridge; they should not tear that up. We all said we would go. We then wasn't loaded; we were all ordered to load, and had strict orders not to fire till they fired first, then to fire as fast as we could. . .

They stayed about ten minutes and then marched back, and we after them. After a while we found them a marching back towards Boston. We was soon after them. When they got about a mile and a half to a road that comes from Bedford and Billerica, they was waylaid and a great many killed. When I got there, a great many lay dead and the road was bloody.

(*Source:* account by Amos Barrett, a member of the Concord minutemen company, April 1775)

The British retreat:

During the whole of the march from Lexington, the Rebels kept an incessant irregular fire from all points of the column, which was more galling as our flanking parties, which at first were placed at sufficient distances to cover the march of it, were at last, from the different obstructions they occasionally met with, obliged to keep almost close to it. Our men had very few opportunities of getting good shots at the Rebels, as they hardly ever fired but under cover of some stone wall, from behind a tree, or out of a house; and the moment they had fired they lay down out of sight until they had loaded again, or the column had passed. In the road indeed in our rear, they were most numerous, and came pretty close, frequently calling out 'King Hancock forever'.

Many of them were killed in the houses on the road side from whence they fired; in some, seven or eight men were destroyed. Some houses were forced open in which no person could be discovered, but when the column had passed, numbers sailed forth from some place in which they had lain concealed, fired at the rear guard, and augmented the numbers which followed us. If we had time to set fire to those houses, many rebels must have perished in them, but as night drew on, Lord Percy thought it best to continue the march. Many houses were plundered by the soldiers, notwithstanding the efforts of the officers to prevent it. I have no doubt that this inflamed the Rebels, and made many of them follow us farther than they otherwise would have done. By all accounts some soldiers who stayed too long in the houses, were killed in the very act of plundering by those who lay concealed in them.

(*Source:* diary of Lieutenant Frederick Mackenzie of the Royal Welsh Fusiliers, April 1775)

MAY 1775   Rebels capture Fort Ticonderoga.

Fort Ticonderoga was a British garrison which guarded the River Hudson-Lake Champlain river passage to Canada. A small rebel force took the fort by surprise before dawn on 10 May. Most importantly, the rebels took charge of the cannon and mortar of the fort. These were hauled across country and in March 1776 were set up on Dorchester Heights, overlooking Boston Harbour.

Second Continental Congress:

On the day Ticonderoga fell a Second Continental Congress met in Philadelphia, with representatives from all thirteen colonies. This body became, in effect, a national government and remained in existence until 1789. It authorised the issuing of a Continental currency and the establishment of a United Colonies Post Office under Benjamin Franklin.

The Continental Army:

At the Congress John Adams proposed that the rebels laying siege to Boston and beginning to push north from Ticonderoga into Canada should be considered the nucleus of a Continental Army. The Congress agreed and appointed George Washington from Virginia, Commander-in-Chief.

A letter from George Washington to his wife, June 1775:

My dearest,

I am now set down to write to you on a subject which fills me with inexpressible concern, and this concern is greatly aggravated and increased, when I reflect upon the uneasiness I know it will cause you. It has been determined in Congress that the whole army raised for the defense of the American cause shall be put under my care, and that it is necessary for me to proceed immediately to Boston to take upon me the command of it.

You may believe me, my dear Patsy, when I assure you in the most solemn manner that, so far from seeking this appointment, I have used every endeavour to avoid it, not only from my unwillingness to part with you and the family, but from a consciousness of its being a trust too great for my capacity, and that I should enjoy more real happiness in one month with you at home than I have the most distant prospect of finding abroad, if my stay were to be seven times seven years. But as it has been a kind of destiny that has thrown me upon this service, I shall hope that my undertaking it is designed to answer some good purpose.

The Continental Army in June was scarcely an army at all. It had to be formed out of the colonial militias, but many of them were unwilling to enlist for three or more years. By the end of 1776 Washington had only 3,000 soldiers under his command. The effective strength of the Continental Army during most of the war was 15,000 men, rising every spring and falling each autumn.

The other armed American force was the rebel militia who fought a guerilla war in their own areas.

Despite its preparations for conflict, the Second Congress attempted to avoid war with Britain. It sent a petition, known as the Olive Branch Petition, to the King, professing loyalty and allegiance to the Crown. It appealed to the King to stop hostilities and repeal all repressive measures since 1763. When the petition reached London in September 1775 George III refused to receive it.

JUNE 1775 Bunker Hill:

In June, New England rebels occupied Breed's Hill and Bunker Hill on the Charlestown peninsula overlooking Boston. The British in Boston had been reinforced by the arrival of new troops and Generals Burgoyne, Clinton and Howe. To prevent a permanent rebel camp being set up on the hills, the British attacked. The rebels were driven away but the British suffered heavy casualties. They were stunned by the rebels' strength and launched no more attacks during the following autumn or winter. General Gage was recalled to London for incompetence and was replaced as Commander-in-Chief by General William Howe.

A report by General Gage:

You will receive an account of some success against the rebels, but attended with a long list of killed and wounded on our side; so many of the latter that the hospital has hardly hands sufficient to take care of them. These people shew a spirit and conduct against us, they never shewed against the French, and every body has judged them from their former appearance, and behaviour, when joyned with the king's forces in the last war; which has led many into great mistakes.

They are now spirited up by a rage and enthusiasm, as great as ever people were possessed of, and you must proceed in earnest or give the business up. A small body acting in one spot, will not avail, you must have large armies, making diversions on different sides, to divide their force.

I don't find one province in appearance better disposed than another, though I think if this army was in New York, that we should find many friends, and be able to raise forces in that province on the side of the Government.

Forecasts of British failure:

It is that kind of war in which even victory will ruin us.

(*Source:* letter from Horace Walpole to H. Mann, May 1775)

Waiving all considerations of right and wrong, I ask is it commonsense to use force toward the Americans? Not 20,000 troops, not treble that number fighting 3,000 miles away from home and supplies could hope to conquer a nation fighting for Liberty.

(*Source:* letter from John Wesley to Lord Dartmouth, June 1775)

THINGS TO DO AND THINK ABOUT:

The British Parliament was generally contemptuous of American fighting qualities. In February 1775 the Earl of Sandwich called American fighters "raw, undisciplined, cowardly men". Can you explain why this does not seem to be the case?

Why did the Second Continental Congress set up a Post Office and issue currency?

List the arguments in favour of the King's refusal to see the Olive Branch Petition.

AUGUST 1775   George III's Proclamation for suppressing Rebellion and Sedition.

The Proclamation declared that many of the King's subjects in North America had been "misled by dangerous and ill-designing men" who were "traitorously preparing, ordering and levying war against Us". It urged loyal subjects to resist these men and to bring information about such traitors to officers of the Crown.

26 OCTOBER 1775 On opening Parliament the King referred to ". . . rebellious war . . . manifestly carried on for the purpose of establishing an independent empire".

JANUARY 1776 The pamphlet *Commonsense*, written by Thomas Paine, was published

"Noddle Island or How are we deceived", published in London in May 1776. The cartoonist showed the British retreat from Boston. Noddle Island was another name for William Island in Boston Harbour. The title of the cartoon contains a pun on "Howe". It is believed that it is the British who are flying flags with an ass and a fool's cap and bells. At the top of the hair the two sides are shooting it out while at the bottom Redcoats march away and others row out to waiting ships.

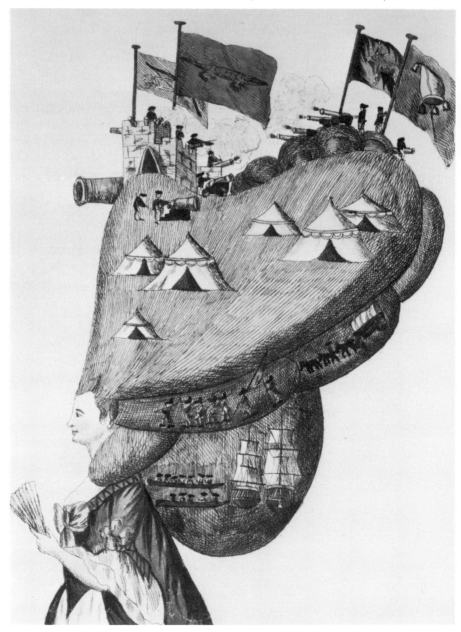

anonymously. It was a blunt and direct argument for independence and was widely read throughout the colonies. Fifty-six editions were printed in just one year. Denying that Americans owed allegiance to "the royal brute of Great Britain", the pamphlet is said to have converted many to the cause of American republicanism.

Everything that is right or natural pleads for separation. The blood of the slain, the weeping voice of nature cries, 'TIS TIME TO PART.
(*Source: Commonsense* by Thomas Paine, 1776)

THINGS TO DO AND THINK ABOUT:

When do you think that war became inevitable between the colonies and Britain?

MARCH 1776 British evacuate Boston.
The guns from Ticonderoga arrived outside Boston in March and the rebels set them up on Dorchester Heights overlooking Boston harbour. General Howe evacuated Boston and withdrew to Halifax, Nova Scotia, leaving behind valuable stores.

MAY 1776 Congress recommends that all colonies should establish their own governments to deal with local affairs.
The power of the Royal Governors collapsed and they withdrew.

JUNE 1776 Congress appoints a committee to draft a Declaration of Independence.
Thomas Jefferson, Benjamin Franklin and John Adams were leading members of the committee.

2 JULY 1776 Congress approves independence.

4 JULY 1776 Declaration of Independence is approved. Independence is declared.

THINGS TO DO AND THINK ABOUT:

Historians disagree about the date of the beginning of the Revolution. When do you think that the American Revolution began? Why?

What were the causes of the American Revolution?

Why do you think that the government did not seek a compromise solution with the American colonies?

Why did the colonists fight for the Revolution?

A wounded soldier at Bunker Hill explained:

I was a Shoemaker, & got my living by my Labor. When this Rebellion came on, I saw some of my Neighbors got into Commission, who were no better than myself. I was very ambitious, & did not like to see those Men above me. I was asked to enlist, as a private Soldier. . . . I offered to enlist upon having a Lieutenant's Commission; which was granted. I imagined myself now in a way of Promotion: if I was killed in Battle, there would be an end of me, but if my Captain was killed, I should rise in Rank, & should still have a Chance to rise higher. These Sir! were the only motives of my entering into the Service; for as to the dispute between Great Britain & the Colonies, I know nothing of it. . .

(*Source:* quoted in *A People's History of the United States* by Howard Zinn, Longman, 1980)

John Adams reported a conversation he had had with an old soldier many years after 1776:

'Captain Preston, why did you go to the Concord fight, the nineteenth of April 1775?' The old man, bowed beneath the weight of years, raised himself upright, and turning to me said 'Why did I go?' 'Yes', I replied. 'My histories tell me that you men of the Revolution took up arms against "intolerable oppressions". What were they?' 'Oppressions. I didn't feel them.' 'What, were you not oppressed by the Stamp Act?' 'I never saw one of those stamps, and always understood that Governor Barnard put them all in Castle William. I am certain I never paid a penny for one of them.' 'Well, what then about the tea tax?' 'Tea tax! I never drank a drop of the stuff – the boys threw it all over board.' 'Then I suppose you had been reading Harrington or Sydney or Locke about the eternal principles of Liberty?' 'Never heard of 'em. We read only the Bible, the Catechism, Wells' Psalms and Hymns and the Almanack'. 'Well, then, what was the matter, and what did you mean in going to the fight?' 'Young man, what we meant in going for those redcoats was this: we always had governed ourselves, and we always meant to. They didn't mean we should'.

(*Source:* quoted in *The War of American Independence*, Esmond Wright, The Historical Association, 1976)

THINGS TO DO AND THINK ABOUT:

From all you have read, why do you think that ordinary men and women supported the American Revolution?

The Result: American Victory or British Failure?

To understand the American Revolution, we must try to form a complete picture of what happened: why and how it started, the course of the Revolution and why it ended as it did. While this book concentrates on events before the Revolution, it would be unsatisfactory not to know what came after.

The result of the American Revolution is as complex as its origins: did the Americans defeat the British or did the British lose because of their own failures? British defeat has been blamed on the size of the American continent, the Atlantic Ocean, poor generals and inadequate supplies, while American success has been attributed mainly to the intervention of the French.

Historians must weigh up the evidence to reach their judgement, but they may not reach the same conclusions. Consider the opinions of two leading historians in their recent books about the American Revolution.

THE VERDICTS **An American victory:**

The English lost, but it took seven years and a world war to beat them. . .

English incompetence helped. It will not do to make too much of this. In terms of ships, men and money, Great Britain put forth a greater effort than she had before, even in the Seven Years War. The war ministers . . . were able and conscientious. . . . The old order in England might be corrupt, but it had always been at its best as a war machine. . . . If British Generals were, at best, merely competent, and were all too often less than that, there was one great Admiral, Rodney. . .

Although in the end, the English had to give up all their holdings in North America south of Canada, they kept their Empire everywhere else. They were defeated, but not conquered.

Still, defeated they were. Partly it was a matter of morale. There was no middle ground for the Americans: for them it was either victory or total submission. They were fighting for their fundamental interests in a way that the British . . . were not.

(*Source: Longman History of the United States of America*, Hugh Brogan, Longman, 1985)

A British failure:

Conduct of the war by the Government was to be marked by sluggishness, negligence, divided counsel and fatal misjudgements of the opponent. Lax management at home translated into lax generalship in the field. . .

Ministers underestimated the task and the needs. Materials and men were inadequate, ships unseaworthy, too few and short of able seamen; problems of transport and communication were unappreciated in London, where direction of the war was retained at a distance that required two or three months for letter and reply . . .

. . . performance was affected by the unpopularity of a war against fellow subjects. . . . The American Revolution, given its own errors and failures . . . succeeded by virtue of British mishandling.

(*Source: The March of Folly*, Barbara Tuchman, Abacus, 1984)

How do the two verdicts differ in their accounts of British defeat?

"The American Revolution . . . succeeded by British mishandling". Do you agree? Why?/Why not?

In one sense, the result of the Revolution could have been predicted in July 1776: colonies which had declared their independence would never again submit willingly to British rule. Britain had forfeited American goodwill by 1776 and would find it impossible to maintain her Empire by force. The British could only win a hollow victory, if a victory at all.

If British observers like Horace Walpole could foresee that a victory could "ruin us", why do you think that the government did not seek a compromise solution with the American colonies?

Sources

PRIMARY SOURCES

Many of the extracts in the book are from primary sources, written during the period of the American Revolution. Of these the most accessible is:

Commonsense, Thomas Paine (The Penguin American Library, 1982)

Many of the documents can be found in collections such as:
English Historical Documents, Volume IX – American Colonial Documents to 1776, M. Jenson (Eyre and Spottiswoode, 1955)

The Fire of Liberty, Esmond Wright (Hamish Hamilton, 1983) In this book Professor Wright presents a large number of British and American accounts and diaries written during the American Revolution.

Statements in Parliament can be found in the relevant volumes of Hansard's *Parliamentary History*. Volumes XVI to XIX deal with the period from January 1765 to December 1778.

RECENT PUBLICATIONS

In preparing this book the author found the following very useful:

1776: The British Story of the American Revolution, Times Newspapers Ltd (Times Books, 1976)
The book is the catalogue of the 1776 exhibition which was held at the National Maritime Museum, Greenwich, in 1976 to mark the bicentenary of the American Revolution. The exhibition told the story of the Revolution from both sides of the Atlantic. The book contains short pieces by several historians, photographs and maps.

Longman History of the United States of America, Hugh Brogan (Longman, 1985)
This is probably the best narrative history of America. Part Two of the book deals with "The old order and the American Revolution".

A History of the United States : 1 The Birth of the U.S.A., R.B. Nye and J.E. Morpurgo (Pelican, 1970)
Another narrative history. It was written as a collaborative effort by an Englishman and an American.

The Age of the Democratic Revolution. Volume 1, R.R. Palmer (Princeton University Press, 1971)
This is a controversial book which attempts to show that the American Revolution was part of a general democratic revolution in the eighteenth century. Palmer deals in detail with British politics and the American Revolution as well as looking at revolutions in Europe including the French Revolution.

The American Revolution, Roger Parkinson (Wayland Pictorial Sources Series, Wayland, 1971)
An interesting collection of many contemporary illustrations.

England in the Eighteenth Century, J.H. Plumb (The Pelican History of England, Pelican, 1973)
Useful for background information on eighteenth-century England.

The March of Folly, Barbara W. Tuchman (Abacus, 1985)
A stimulating book which concentrates on three examples of governments which followed policies contrary to their own interests. One of the examples is the British government's folly in losing its American Empire.

The American War of Independence, Peter Wells (Hodder and Stoughton, 1978)
A thorough and useful survey of the events from 1763 to 1783, from British and American viewpoints.

Biographies

THE AMERICANS

ADAMS John (1735-1826): lawyer, rebel, and second President of the United States of America

John Adams studied law at Harvard and was called to the bar in Boston, Massachusetts, in 1758. He took some part in town politics and became well-known for his opposition to the Stamp Act.

In 1770 he defended the British soldier, Captain Preston, for his part in the Boston Massacre. This did not make him popular among more radical Americans and Adams withdrew from politics until he joined in the protests against the Intolerable Acts of 1773. A cautious man, Adams was only slowly reconciled to a break from Britain. He was one of the Massachusetts delegates to the First Continental Congress and in the Second Congress he seconded Lee's motion for independence.

From 1778 to 1788 he represented America in France, Holland and Britain where he became the first ambassador of the United States in London.

When John Adams returned to America he served two terms as Vice-President to George Washington, from 1789 to 1792 and from 1792 to 1796, before becoming the second President of the United States in 1796. His son, John Quincy Adams, became President in 1825.

FRANKLIN Benjamin (1706-90): printer, author, inventor, scientist, statesman and diplomat

Benjamin Franklin was born in Boston, the tenth son of a soapmaker. He became educated mainly through his own efforts and was apprenticed as a printer.

By the age of twenty-four Franklin owned a printing works in Philadelphia and was rich enough to retire in 1748.

His interests were wide: he was a natural scientist; he experimented with electricity and invented a lightning conductor; in Philadelphia he ran the *Pennsylvania Gazette*, and his *Poor Richard's Almanac* sold 10,000 copies annually; he pioneered a volunteer firefighting society; he established the first circulating library and an academy which grew to be the University of Pennsylvania. In 1748 Franklin entered the Pennsylvanian assembly and was Pennsylvania's London agent from 1757.

In the years before the revolution Franklin attempted to represent American interests to the British Parliament and people. He favoured conciliation between Britain and her colonies but was a rebel by 1775.

On his return to America in 1775 Franklin was chosen as a delegate to the Second Continental Congress and was a member of the committee which drafted the Declaration of Independence. Between 1776 and 1785 Franklin worked to promote the American cause in France and was a major influence behind the American-French Treaty of 1778.

From 1785 to 1788 Franklin served as president of the executive council of Philadelphia, and at the age of 81, in 1787, was a member of the Constitutional Convention, to create a constitution for the United States of America.

HENRY Patrick (1736-99): lawyer and rebel

Patrick Henry was an unsuccessful store-keeper who became a lawyer in 1760.

As a member of the Virginian assembly he introduced radical resolutions in opposition to the Stamp Act and was widely accepted as a leader of Virginian radicals from 1765. With Thomas Jefferson and Richard Henry Lee, he initiated the committees of correspondence to coordinate rebel action. He also led the call for armed resistance with his famous cry of "Give me liberty or give me death". From 1774 to 1776 Henry was a member of the Continental Congress and served two terms as governor of Virginia from 1776-79 and 1784-86.

Once the constitution of the United States had been agreed, Henry returned to his law practice, declining offers of appointments as senator, secretary of state and chief justice.

JEFFERSON Thomas (1743-1826): lawyer, rebel and third President of the United States of America

Thomas Jefferson was born into a well-off family of Virginian plantation owners with important social and political connections. He trained and practised as a lawyer until the revolution. Jefferson became a member of the Virginian assembly in 1769 and a member of the Continental Congress in 1775. A friend of Patrick Henry's, he was anti-British from quite early in his political career. His pamphlet *A summary view of the rights of British America*, published in 1774, fell just short of calling for independence.

He was only thirty-three when asked by Congress to draft the Declaration of Independence. The document was amended by John Adams and Benjamin

Franklin but most of Jefferson's phrases survived.

Thomas Jefferson was governor of Virginia 1779-81; member of Congress 1783-85; ambassador in Paris 1784-89; secretary of state 1790-93; Vice-President 1797-1801; and President 1801-9.

WASHINGTON George (1732-99): surveyor, soldier and first President of the United States of America

George Washington was born in Virginia, the eldest son of a plantation owner. He began his working life as a surveyor and took many acres of unclaimed land for himself. He also inherited wealth and by the age of twenty-one was rich, a landowner and a major in the Virginia militia. In the militia Washington was involved in the defence of the frontier from French and Indian attacks. Washington married in 1759 and settled on his estate at Mount Vernon.

As a member of the Virginian assembly he changed his opinions slowly from loyalty to Britain to open rebellion against British rule. He played a leading role in opposing the Townsend duties and the Intolerable Acts.

Washington was elected as one of the Virginian delegates to the Continental Congress and was appointed Commander-in-Chief of the Continental Army in 1775. In the war of independence he kept his army together despite hardships and lack of supplies. He resigned his commission in December 1783 and returned to Mount Vernon but was recalled to public life as president of the Philadelphia Convention in 1787.

George Washington became the first President of the United States of America in 1789, was re-elected in 1792 and declined a third term of office in 1796. Before retiring he gave a Farewell Address to the Nation in which he emphasized the importance of a strong union of states and a powerful central government.

Sources for "The Americans"

Concise Dictionary of American Biography, Managing Editor: Joseph Hopkins (Charles Scribner's Sons New York and O.U.P., 1964)

1776: The British Story of the American Revolution, Times Newspapers Ltd (Times Books, 1976)

The American War of Independence, Peter Wells (Hodder and Stoughton, 1978)

THE BRITISH

BURKE Edmund (1729-97): lawyer, writer and Member of Parliament

Edmund Burke was born in Ireland and educated at Trinity College, Dublin. He left for London in 1750 and entered the Middle Temple but soon left the legal profession to concentrate on literary work. Although he lacked family connections and wealth, Burke found a patron in the 2nd Earl of Vinney and, with his help, entered Parliament as member for Wendover and a Whig in 1765. Burke worked as private secretary to the Marquess of Rockingham, a leading Opposition Whig from 1766 to 1782.

The power of the Whigs had declined in Parliament since George III had come to the throne. Burke believed that Parliament was being undermined by the patronage of the King and his use of the "King's Men". Burke became well-known for his political pamphlets. His major criticism of the government came in his pamphlet *Thoughts on the Present Discontents,* written in response to the Wilkes case. He also took an active part in debates on affairs in America. Burke believed in the liberty of each American. On 22 March 1775 he spoke for three hours in the House of Commons on the need for peaceful conciliation with the colonists. He was heavily defeated. Burke also denounced the British use of American Indians in the war and supported the abolition of the slave trade in 1778. In his opposition to the French Revolution in 1789, Burke appeared as a champion of the old ruling class but he was simply suspicious of the methods of the French revolutionaries: he never disapproved of the cause of liberty.

GEORGE III (1738-1820)

George III came to the throne in 1760 at the age of twenty-two. As King he attempted to break the power of the Whigs and recover more influence for the throne, although he declared himself in favour of the constitutional monarchy. The King supported his Parliament in their quarrels with the American colonies and contemplated abdication rather than recognizing the independence of the United States.

He was a popular King and a cultured man. He was a patron of literature, art, science and music. His library, now in the British Museum, was freely available to scholars and was for a long time the only national library. He collected works of art and founded the Royal Academy of Arts. He was interested in science and commissioned the great telescope. Nicknamed "Farmer George", he practised scientific farming.

George III was a deeply religious man and enjoyed his family life; he had nine sons and six daughters. His first attack of insanity happened in 1765; more attacks followed in 1788 and 1803. Eventually, George III became blind and after 1811 was permanently deranged. His son acted as regent until 1820.

LORD NORTH (1732-92): First Minister

Francis, Lord North, who later succeeded to the family title as the 2nd Earl of Guildford, entered the House of Commons at the age of twenty-two. He became Chancellor of the Exchequer in 1767 and First Minister in 1770. North refused to call himself Prime Minister as he declared that no such title existed in the British constitution. He held office for twelve years but realized that he was not a capable war minister. He once declared: "Upon military matters, I speak ignorantly, and therefore without effect." After the battle at Saratoga North tried to resign but the King refused and continued to refuse to accept North's offers of resignation throughout the American war of independence. The King realized that another Minister might challenge his own political role.

North was expert at controlling the business of the House of Commons and was highly skilled in matters concerning the Treasury. He was relieved to leave office five months after the fall of Yorktown.

PAINE Thomas (1737-1809): staymaker, excise officer, teacher, writer and revolutionary

Tom Paine was born in Thetford, Norfolk, in 1737. After being educated in the village school he was apprenticed to his father's shop to learn the trade of making women's corsets. At the age of nineteen he left Thetford and for the next twelve years moved around the country working as a staymaker, excise officer and teacher. Paine's first wife died in 1760 and he was soon separated from his second wife.

Having been dismissed from his work as an excise man because of leading the agitation for a pay increase, Paine was separated, jobless and without money and so decided to try his luck in America. He obtained a letter of introduction from Benjamin Franklin and travelled to America where he began work as a teacher. Paine was soon persuaded to write for the *Pennsylvania Magazine*. He wrote many short pieces including an attack on slavery and a plea for women's rights. In January 1776 his pamphlet *Commonsense* was published anonymously. It urged independence for America and was an immediate success.

In July 1776 Paine enlisted in the American army and combined the role of soldier with that of writer. He wrote a series of pamphlets to maintain American morale. They were later published together as *The Crisis*.

Paine was in France at the beginning of the French Revolution in 1789, and was greeted as a hero of the American Revolution. He remained in France for the next ten years, unable to return to Britain as he had been outlawed, in his absence, because of the revolutionary ideas on government and religion expressed in his books, *The Rights of Man* and *The Age of Reason*. In 1802 he returned to America but his role in the Revolution had been largely forgotten.

PITT William (1708-78): politician and statesman

William Pitt, who became the Earl of Chatham in 1766, was also known as "the Elder Pitt" and "the Great Commoner". The youngest son of an undistinguished family, he married into one of the greatest Whig families, that of Temple of Stowe. He entered Parliament in 1735 and made his name by brilliant patriotic speeches.

He was unpopular with the King, George II, but because of Whig influence, he became Paymaster-General and a privy councillor in 1746. His political career was brilliant but varied as he had periods in and out of office. He became Secretary of State and Leader of the House of Commons in 1757. During the Seven Years War he was in control of foreign and military affairs and helped to guide Britain to victory in 1763.

Once George III came to the throne Pitt's power declined. He opposed attempts to tax the American colonies and demanded that Britain should continue only to regulate trade.

In August 1766 Pitt, now in the House of Lords as Lord Chatham, became First Minister, but for the two years of his office he was close to physical collapse because of illness, and he was not in control of policies or colleagues. Pitt opposed policies to withdraw completely from America. In April 1778 he collapsed in the Lords while speaking against withdrawal. He died a month later.

Sources for "The British"

1776: The British Story of the American Revolution, Times Newspapers Ltd (Times Books, 1976)

The American War of Independence, Peter Wells (Hodder and Stoughton, 1978)

Webster's Biographical Dictionary (G.C. Merriam and Co, 1966)

Commonsense (The introduction to the Penguin edition, edited by Isaac Kramnick, The Penguin American Library, 1982)

Glossary

abatis	a defence made by placing felled trees lengthwise one over the other with their branches towards the enemy's line.
absolved	set free
actuated	motivated
arbitrary	based on mere opinion or preference
boycott	refusal to buy certain goods
citadel	a fortress usually overlooking a city which it protects and dominates
colony	a settlement in a new country whose settlers are still connected politically with their parent state
commission	the warrant by which an officer in the armed forces is appointed to a rank
deficit	an excess of money spent over the amount of income
delegate	a person sent to act for or represent others
despotism	a political system under the authority of an absolute ruler
Dominions	all territories under British control
duty	a payment to the public revenue, especially one levied on the import and export of goods
excise	a duty charged on home goods during manufacture or before their sale to home consumers
flank	the extreme right or left side of an army on the march
forfeited	given up as a penalty
freeborn	born to the conditions and privileges of citizenship and inheriting liberty
hireling	one who serves in return for money
husbandry	the business of agriculture and farming
imperial	associated with the system of empire
inalienable	that cannot be transferred
indentured servant	servant bound by contract to serve a master for a number of years, in return for only his/her keep and, in this case, a passage to America. When the contract expired, the servant was a free man or woman
legislator	one who makes laws; a member of a law-making body
loyalist	one who continues to support the existing form of government
magazines	buildings for storing the arms, ammunition and provisions of an army
mercenary	soldier working in a foreign army
militia	an army of citizens, not a body of professional soldiers
monopoly	the exclusive privilege of selling some commodity or of trading with a particular place or country
New England	the six north eastern colonies of America
parliamentary privilege	certain immunities from prosecution granted to Members of Parliament
perquisites	money in addition to salary; almost a "tip"
pomatum	a scented ointment for application to the skin
portmanteaux	bags or cases
radical	one who has advanced views on political issues
rapine	robbery
rectitude	righteousness, goodness, correctness
Republic	a state in which the supreme power rests in the people and their elected representatives and there is no monarch

retrenchment	last line of defence
sovereignty	supremacy in power and authority
statutes	decrees
transient	temporary
usurpation	unlawful seizure of power
veteran	an experienced soldier
vindicate	to rescue
Yankee	a nickname for a New-Englander and also used for an American of the northern states

Date List

1760	Accession of George III.
1763	End of Seven Years War and the Peace of Paris.
1764	Sugar Act.
1765 March **October**	Stamp Act. Stamp Act Congress meets.
1766 March	Repeal of the Stamp Act. Declaratory Act.
1767 June	Townsend duties.
1770 January **March** **April**	Lord North becomes Prime Minister. Boston Massacre. Townsend duties abolished except for tax on tea.
1772 June	*Gaspee* incident.
1773 May **December**	Tea Act. Boston Tea Party.
1774 March-June **September**	Intolerable Acts. First Continental Congress.
1775 April **May** **June** **August**	Lexington and Concord. Rebels capture Fort Ticonderoga. Second Continental Congress. George Washington appointed Commander-in-Chief of the Continental Army. Olive Branch Petition sent to London. Battle of Bunker Hill. George III's Proclamation for suppressing Rebellion and Sedition.
1776 January **March** **July** **September** **December**	*Commonsense* published. British evacuate Boston. Declaration of Independence. British occupy New York. British occupy Rhode Island. Washington retreats into Pennsylvania, then crosses Delaware River and wins victory at Trenton.
1777 January	Washington defeats British at Princeton.

September	British defeat Washington's troops at Brandywine, and occupy Philadelphia.
October	British troops under Burgoyne surrender at Saratoga.
	Washington spends winter at Valley Forge.
1778 February	France signs Treaty of Alliance with the Rebels.
June	British, under Clinton, evacuate Philadelphia.
June 28	Battle of Monmouth.
July	French fleet arrives off New York.
December	British occupy Savannah, Georgia.
1779 June	Spain declares war on Britain.
August	French fleet in English Channel threatens invasion of Britain.
	American ship off coast of Britain.
1780 May	British capture Charlestown, South Carolina.
1780 August	Rebels' defeat at Camden.
1781 January	British defeat at Cowpens.
March	British win victory at Guildford Court House.
October	Cornwallis surrenders his army after siege of Yorktown.
1782 March	Lord North resigns; succeeded by a Whig coalition under Rockingham.
April	Battle of the Saints.
July	British evacuate Savannah.
	On Rockingham's death Shelbourne forms government.
November	Preliminary Articles of Peace agreed in Paris.
December	British evacuate Charlestown.
1783 February	British and Americans declare the cessation of hostilities.
September	Treaty of Paris signed.
November	Final evacuation of New York.
1785 June	John Adams becomes first Ambassador of the United States of America to Great Britain.

Index